No Turning Back

An Exposition of the Epistle to the Hebrews

No Turning Back

An Exposition of the Epistle to the Hebrews

by

J. Philip Arthur

GRACE PUBLICATIONS TRUST
175 Tower Bridge Road
London SE1 2AH
England
e-mail: AGBCSE@AOL.com

Joint Managing Editors:
T. I. Curnow
D.P. Kingdon MA, BD

Consulting Editor:
J. Philip Arthur MA

Unless otherwise indicated Scripture quotations are taken from the HOLY BIBLE, The New King James Version, ©1983 by Thomas Nelson, Inc., Nashville, TN USA. Used by permission.

Distributed by
EVANGELICAL PRESS
Faverdale North Industrial Estate
Darlington
DL3 OPH
England

British Library Cataloguing in Publication Data available

ISBN 0 946462-64-X

Printed and bound in Great Britain by
Creative Print & Design Wales, Ebbw Vale, NP3 5SD

Contents

It is a great asset to a minister of the
gospel to have a praying mother.
This book is dedicated to mine.

Far off I see the goal;
O Saviour guide me;
I feel my strength is small;
Be thou beside me:
With vision ever clear,
With love that conquers fear,
And grace to persevere,
O Lord provide me.

Whene'er Thy way seems strange,
Go Thou before me;
And, lest my heart should change,
O Lord, watch o'er me;
But should my faith prove frail,
And I through blindness fail,
O let Thy grace prevail,
And still restore me.

Should earthly pleasure wane,
And joy forsake me,
If lonely hours of pain
At length o'ertake me,
My hand in Thine hold fast
Till sorrow be o'erpast,
And gentle death at last
For heaven awake me.

There with the ransomed throng
Who praise for ever
The love that made them strong
To serve for ever,
I too would see Thy face,
Thy finished work retrace,
And magnify Thy grace,
Redeemed for ever.

Robert Rowland Roberts (1865-1945)

Preface

Whenever people who have been Christians for some time get together, the conversation often turns to friends that they had in common years ago. It is not unusual for someone to ask, 'What about so and so? How is he getting on?' It is also depressingly common to discover that the person in question no longer makes any pretence of being a Christian. Someone who began well no longer attends church, no longer associates with Christian people and rapidly changes the subject when spiritual matters come up in conversation. It almost seems that the phenomenon of the temporary disciple is a common feature of the contemporary Evangelical scene. I have encountered this situation many times myself. Recent visits to the Philippines also made it forcibly clear that in some parts of the Third World that have been influenced by Western Evangelicalism the same problem is perhaps even more acute. The message of the epistle to the Hebrews is especially appropriate to the modern scene. It was originally addressed to people who were considering going back on their profession of faith in Christ. It encourages them to persevere by holding Jesus up Christ before them. Christians have a great salvation because they have a great Saviour! He makes perseverance worthwhile. It was this that made me think about turning a series of sermons, originally preached in 1992, into a modest book.

This little volume is not intended to be an exhaustive commentary. It does not set out to provide close and careful analysis of every part of the text of the epistle. There are already a number of books that achieve this purpose very well. Several are mentioned in the appendix at the back of this book. My purpose in writing is to give a reasonably comprehensive exposition of the epistle without going into too much detail in the hope that this might make the message of the epistle accessible to people in a wide variety of situations. I believe that this book of the Bible has an urgent and compelling message for today's Christians. If I have helped a little towards allowing the book to speak for itself I will be amply rewarded. Whether I have succeeded in this task, others must judge.

I am very grateful to the long-suffering congregation at Free Grace Baptist Church at Lancaster in the North West of England for the patient hearing they gave the original sermons and to John Appleby and Philip Grist, then of Grace Publications Trust and Grace Baptist Mission respectively, for suggesting that my material might have the makings of a book. I owe Margaret Siddans a considerable debt. She went over my first draft with scrupulous care and made numerous helpful suggestions aimed at making the English more straightforward, just in case the end product should ever stray into the hands of believers who have English as their second language. This book has actually had a gestation period of several years. More recently I have been encouraged by the positive and supportive suggestions of Maciek Stolarski of Grace Baptist Mission. He appeared to feel that it was worth persevering when I almost despaired of it ever seeing the light of day. I am also grateful to David Kingdon of Grace Publications Trust for all his editorial work and to an anonymous member of the readers' panel who offered many suggestions that drove me back to the text of the epistle. I am grateful for all his comments and have adopted almost all of them. Scripture quotations, unless otherwise stated, are taken from the New King James Version of the Holy Scriptures.

My wife, Barbara, has done more to keep me sane and useful than anyone will ever know. She deserves much credit for anything that I ever achieve in the Lord's service. The blame for the many imperfections of this book rests with me and me alone. But if, in the course of time, it helps bring one soul an inch nearer the kingdom of God, or helps one of Christ's dear children to a more complete understanding of a small portion of the vast treasure-hoard of Scripture, the effort involved in writing it will have been amply rewarded.

J. Philip Arthur
December 2002

1
AN INTRODUCTION TO THE EPISTLE

Jesus Christ himself is the theme of this epistle. The actual form of the letter is a series of comparisons. The author brings a number of persons and ceremonies before us so that we can compare them with Jesus. As a result we see that he is greater than all of them. Angels, prophets, Moses, Aaron and the priesthood, all are as nothing compared to the Son of God.

As we shall see, the epistle is full of his glory. In order to appreciate this, however, we need to get certain things clear from the beginning.

Who wrote the Epistle?

There is no certain answer to this question. The author has not included his name in the letter. The Authorised Version of the Scriptures ascribes it to the apostle Paul. Many believers favour this idea. Certainly there is no major disagreement between the teachings of Paul and the doctrines contained in Hebrews. Nevertheless, it is unlikely that Paul wrote it.

1. Look at 2:3. Here the author says that both he and the first readers of this letter heard the gospel from people who had themselves heard it from the Lord Jesus Christ in person. Now consider Galatians 1:11-12. Here Paul tells us that he did not hear the gospel from an intermediary but from Jesus himself.

2. The author has a different style from that of Paul. Paul's usual method was to begin with doctrine and then move on to practical and pastoral matters. In Hebrews however, the author does not have two distinct sections, one outlining teaching about the gospel and the other explaining how this should affect our lives. Instead, both are mixed together throughout the letter.

3. One of the most impressive features of the different books of the New Testament is the way that they complement one another. The Holy Spirit prompted the various authors to emphasise different aspects of the same central truths so that, taken together, they make a seamless whole. This is apparent, for instance, in the case of the four gospels, where the individual authors approach the life of Jesus from different perspectives, which, nevertheless, give us a wonderfully complete picture of the life of our Saviour. In the same way, the author of the epistle to the Hebrews, writing to address a situation that does not arise to the same degree in any of Paul's letters, teaches lessons that do not arise in Paul's writings. One area of difference between Paul and the author of this epistle concerns the subject of faith. Paul, for his part, writes of faith chiefly in the sense of personal commitment to Christ. The believer entrusts himself to all that Christ is and all that Christ has done for his people in his substitutionary life and death. This understanding of faith is not entirely absent in Hebrews. The kind of faith that takes hold of the salvation that Christ has bought for us is in view in 10:22 and 10:39. Even so, faith is portrayed in a different way in Chapter 11, where it is described as the ability to perceive a reality that is hidden from our physical senses. If Paul emphasised faith in what God in Christ has done in the past, the author to the Hebrews complements this by reminding us of another dimension of faith that launches out into an unknown future confident that God will provide.

There are one or two things that we can deduce about the author. He had a detailed knowledge of the Old Testament, and the Jewish system of religion. This suggests that he was a converted Jew. He also wrote good Greek. These things led Martin Luther to think that the author may well have been Apollos. We meet this man in Acts 18:24-28. The fact that he was *mighty in the Scriptures*, fervent *in spirit* and an accurate and painstaking teacher suggest that he might have had the necessary qualities. Others have suggested that Barnabas might have been the author. He came from Cyprus, and so would also be skilled in Greek.

There have been occasions in the history of the Christian Church when uncertainty about authorship has led some scholars to question whether this epistle should be included in the canon of Scripture. But even though the identity of the author is known only to God, the subject matter of the epistle is completely in agreement with Apostolic truth. For instance, it includes many strong statements about both the divine and the human natures of Christ. In the end, although we cannot be certain who wrote the words we can be confident that he was inspired by the Holy Spirit. The content of the letter is what is truly important. After all, it is a message from God. It deserves our best attention.

To whom was the Epistle written?

The title makes it clear that this letter was not written to people converted to Christ from a pagan background. These Christians were ethnic Jews who had once practised the Jewish religion. The epistle is full of detailed observations about Old Testament history. The author mentions several incidents and characters from the story of ancient Israel, some prominent, others less so. He also says a great deal about the temple, the sacrifices, the priesthood and so on. He assumes that his readers are familiar with this information. This was their world. These were the traditions that nurtured them. These people were Christians, but Christians who were thoroughly acquainted with Judaism.

It has even been argued that the people in question were from a priestly background, because of the many references to the sacrificial system. We cannot be dogmatic here, but it is worth reminding ourselves that many priests had been converted because of the testimony of the early believers (see Acts 6:7).

It is probable that the epistle was written at a time when the whole Jewish system was still intact. In AD 70 the Romans besieged and sacked Jerusalem and destroyed the temple. This brought an end to the sacrifices and they have never resumed. For this reason Judaism today is very different from the religion that Jesus knew. Then it was a religion of the blood-stained altar and burnt carcasses. Nowadays the ritual of sacrifice has no place in Judaism, which is mainly a religion based around a complex system of ethics. But when this letter was written, the sacrificial system was still functioning. The clue is in 8:13. We read here that the Old Covenant was *becoming obsolete* and was *ready to vanish away*. It would seem that the awful events of AD 70 had not yet unfolded. The old way had been super-seded, but it continued to function at least for the time being.

Why was the Epistle written?

The author was concerned for his readers. They were facing a difficult spiritual challenge. 10:32-34 is very helpful at this point.

It tells us about the *former days*. When the first readers of this letter became Christians they had received a real baptism of fire. Things had been extremely testing and they responded impressively.

1. They knew what it meant to receive scorn and ridicule.

2. Their property had been stolen and damaged.

3. They had been willing to stand by fellow believers who were being persecuted, including the author himself during a time in prison. This was a brave thing to do. It would have made people notice, and brought more persecution down upon them.

We can only admire these first century Christians. They had paid a heavy price for their loyalty to the Saviour. However, even as he paid tribute to their devotion, the writer sadly observed that things had changed. They had gone back. This is apparent in 5:12-14. The decline was so startling that it resembled a fully grown adult returning to babyhood. The author describes one of the symptoms in 10:25. They no longer met together regularly. (That is a good test of a person's spiritual temperature even today).

What concerned the author was that his readers were showing alarming signs of repeating the errors of their ancestors. When Israel left Egypt they began well, but soon rebelled against God in the wilderness. Throughout their history the Jewish people had demonstrated an alarming tendency to turn their backs on God after a period of blessing. That is why this letter contains a number of strong warnings about the danger of falling away from a profession of faith in Christ. There is no doubt that the writer was in earnest. He expresses one of his warnings in the strongest terms (see 6:4-6). Let the readers take courage and press on!

What was the problem that confronted these people? It was a great crisis. They deserve our sympathy. At the root of it all was their Jewishness. They had a religious heritage that had no equal in the ancient world. It was something to be a Jew. In so many ways they were better off than their pagan neighbours.

1. Not for the Jews the worship of countless minor gods and goddesses. At the centre of their faith was a loyal attachment to the worship of the one true and living God.

2. Israel had the law given to Moses. Which other nation could claim such an impressive code of ethics?

3. Jewish worship had no rival. Its core was the solemn ritual of the temple. It was awe-inspiring and spine-tingling. It offered religious spectacle of the highest order. There was music, incense, singing, the ordered movements of the priests, and the high drama of the sacrifices.

4. Heroes and martyrs had suffered for this faith. The revolt of the Maccabees against the pagan tyrant Antiochus Ephiphanes in the second century BC was still fresh in the memories of devout Jews.

Who would want to reject a heritage like theirs? Religion and patriotism were bound together. Similar situations sometimes arise in today's world. For example, many citizens of the Irish Republic would be extremely reluctant to consider converting to Protestantism. For Irishmen of nationalist and republican sympathies, rejecting Roman Catholicism would amount to a betrayal of their national identity. In a similar way these Jewish Christians had no wish to cut themselves off from their roots.

Sadly a cruel dilemma faced them. Was it not possible to be a Jew and a follower of Jesus at the same time? In theory this

was possible. Their faith in Christ was the fulfilment of Judaism.
This, however, was something that the Jewish world would not
permit. The book of Acts shows us several examples of Jewish
hostility to the gospel. Jesus experienced it, and so did many of
his disciples. As far as the Jewish authorities were concerned, it
was a fight to the finish. For Jewish Christians, therefore, life
would have been much easier if they could have made their
peace with the Jewish community, and return to familiar friendships and loyalties. Perhaps they deceived themselves that they
could still hang on to their Christianity, but keep it quiet, adopt
a low profile and remain inconspicuous. This was the one thing
that the Jewish community would never allow them to do. If
they were to come back into the Jewish fold they would have
to renounce Christianity. The Epistle to the Hebrews is written
to a group of people facing this temptation. The author was
able to see just how serious the issues were. He spelled it out
for them in 10:29:

1. It would amount to trampling *the Son of God underfoot*.
When a Jew became a Christian he confessed that 'Jesus is
Lord'. This meant that Jesus was Jehovah, the God of the Old
Testament. A return to Judaism meant saying that this was
untrue. It involved a deliberate and conscious denial of Jesus
as the Son of God.

2. It also meant denying that there was any virtue in the
blood of the covenant. Jesus' blood was nothing special. It
achieved nothing, and it was a delusion to suppose that it could
reconcile anyone to God.

3. It involved a calculated insult to the *Spirit of grace*. If you
say to God that you have no need of the blood of Jesus, you
say that you have no need of forgiveness. You can manage
without grace. It is to hear God's offer of pardon and then act
as if you have not heard it.

Many a follower of Jesus has done as Peter did and denied his Lord, only to repent and find restoration. It is quite another matter to deliberately renounce one's profession of Christianity on a permanent basis. That is to run the risk of apostasy. Truly, *It is a fearful thing to fall into the hands of the living God* (10:31). Has this epistle anything to say to Christians living in the early twentyfirst century? Few modern Christians have Jewish blood in their veins! Even so, it is a letter for us. Believers today are still tempted to fall short of their profession. The backslider is by no means extinct. Christianity still claims that Jesus is unique. It still confronts the world with the daring assertion that he is *the way, the truth, and the life* (John 14:6). It says that without Christ we cannot be reconciled to God. The gospel challenges all other faiths and philosophies. There is a price to pay for maintaining a Christian testimony in the twenty-first century as much as in the first. We face the same test that Christians faced then. It is the temptation to duck beneath the parapet, so to speak, and avoid the flying bullets. The pressure is always on to become a dumb Christian, a disciple in private, but not in public. We, too, sometimes heed the treacherous inner voice that asks whether it is really worth all the aggravation. Wouldn't it be better just to give it all up?

What is the Epistle's message to wavering Christians?

Hebrews has much to say to such people. There are stern warnings. There are sharp exhortations to believers to grow up and act their spiritual age. There is also the challenge to imitate the faith of the giants of the past. At times the author reminds his readers that although they made a good beginning, they still need to persevere. Above all, he presents one clear and unambiguous message again and again: consider Jesus! (see 12:3).

This epistle is full of Christ. Discouraged Christians cannot do better than take a journey through its pages, for over and over again it will bring them face to face with Jesus. We shall meet him as the man who shares our humanity and knows what we are going through. He knows human experience from the inside. We shall encounter him as the great High Priest who has dealt with our sin by dying in our place, the one who has opened up a new and living way so that we can approach God with confidence. He is the One who will not lose a single true believer. In this book we shall find the only friend who never stops praying for us. A journey through Hebrews is an encounter with the One who makes the struggle worth it!

2
JESUS – GOD'S FINAL WORD TO MANKIND

Please read Hebrews 1:1-3

Introduction

Hebrews is a message from God. It was first sent to Christians of Jewish extraction in the first century. Here were people under pressure. All around them voices were urging them to come home to the faith of their ancestors. With this in mind the author wastes no time. There is no opening greeting. Instead he begins immediately on his great theme: the supremacy of Christ! He must make these Hebrews see that there is no comparison between following Jesus and the thought-world of Judaism that they had left behind. If they returned to Judaism, they would find that they had rejected something so much better.

Today's churches need to hear the same message. A bewildering variety of religious options is open to modern people. Does it really make a difference? Is it not arrogance to say that Jesus surpasses all his rivals? This epistle urges us to have confidence in him. He is God's final revelation to men.

How God spoke to the Fathers (1)

Jews have always believed that God is a God who speaks. He revealed himself to their ancestors. Christians share this view:

God sent the prophets to ancient Israel. This is exciting. Most religions teach that human beings must search for God. How sad and futile it all is. Because of sin there is a barrier that cannot be penetrated. Strenuous spiritual effort and mental discipline cannot break through. However hard we try to find a way through to him, we could never know God through our own unaided efforts. The good news however is that God can be known. This is because he speaks. He has not left men and women in ignorance about himself or what it takes to begin and then enjoy a relationship with him.

At first he spoke through human intermediaries, the prophets (see 2 Peter 1:21). Let us be clear that this revelation was accurate. It is sometimes suggested that because God spoke through fallible men, the message itself was therefore fallible. This is unworthy of God. *It is impossible for God to lie* (6:18), and, as God said to Moses: *Who has made man's mouth?* (Exodus 4:11). God must speak the truth. He is the truth! According to Psalm 12:6, *The words of the* LORD *are pure words, like silver tried in a furnace of earth, purified seven times.* This means that he never communicates a revelation in a mixture of true and false statements.

On the other hand we need to understand that the revelation God gave to the prophets, while true and clear, was not complete. God had not said all that he was going to say. God revealed himself 'bit by bit'. No single prophet spoke the entire mind of God. Each one added to the picture. Some had much to say (Isaiah wrote 66 chapters), others said little. Nevertheless, each one brought a message from God, yet none of them, not even all of them together, left God with nothing further to say to the human race.

God spoke through the prophets *at various times.* Altogether it took more than a thousand years, as stage by stage he gave the light. He showed to Abraham the great principle of atonement through the death of a substitute. He gave Moses the

Law. Isaiah learned of the coming servant who would suffer for his people. Each development added to what had gone before, yet when Malachi, the last of the prophets put down his pen, God had not finished. Some important truths were as yet unknown.

God also revealed himself through the prophets *in different ways*. There is no typical prophet; each one was a person with his own background and temperament. The same God was speaking, but there was variety in the way that his message came across. Amos thundered; Jeremiah wept. Sometimes the message was a call to repentance, at other times it was one of comfort and encouragement. At times God gave a sight of his purposes unfolding into the far distant future. The whole revelation was much too great for any one person to convey in one manner.

The Hebrew Christians who were the first readers of this Epistle lived at a watershed in human history. Things had changed. God had revealed himself to their ancestors through the prophets, but that was *in time past*. The prophets had served their God-given purpose, and God had begun to do something new.

How God speaks to us (2)

Now, said the author, God had spoken to his people through his Son. It was the same God who spoke. This was something those troubled Christians needed to grasp. It was easy to listen to Jews claiming that they had deserted God because they had left the prophets behind. The point is that God had more to say. His disclosure of himself through the prophets and through his Son go together. We need both Testaments if we are to enjoy the complete picture. A Christian who ignores the Old Testament neglects God's own introductory revelation. Worse still, the Jew who neglects the New Testament deprives himself of the conclusion. The Old Testament prepares us for the coming of Christ. In the New Testament he comes to us!

The author wanted his readers to see that Jesus is himself a message from God. In sending his Son into the world God was saying something. Those Hebrew believers had done well to take Jesus seriously, but if they should turn away from him they would be shutting their ears to God. We too must understand the situation. Jesus deserves our best attention. His teaching, his life, death and resurrection are, taken together, God's final word to humanity. If we leave Jesus out of the reckoning we are, in fact, allowing God's message to us to fall on deaf ears.

Note the expression, *in these last days*. The Greek can be read 'in the end of these days'. The Jews of that period used two expressions to convey their understanding of time. First of all there was the period covering world history up until the coming of the Messiah. Thus when God speaks to mankind through his Son, he does so '... in the end of these days'. An age is closing. The endless, limitless 'age of Messiah' has dawned. God has no more to say because his purposes have been accomplished. When God spoke through the prophets he left certain things unsaid. Almost two thousand years have rolled by, but the end is imminent. We too live 'in the end of these days'. In Jesus, God has spoken his final word. Let us pay attention to it!

The Son through whom God speaks (2-3)

The Son supersedes the prophets because he is far greater. Our passage tells us several things about him:

First of all, he is the *heir of all things*. He is the heir because he is the Son. He is intimately related to the Father. The idea here is not that God the Father must die one day. God is immortal. Rather, what belongs to the Father also belongs as of right to the Son. What are the 'all things'? The answer is found in Colossians 1:19-20. Jesus is the heir of the things that he is to reconcile to God. In particular this includes redeemed people. Look at Psalm 2:7-8. Why did God pardon your sin? He did so in order that he might give you to Jesus! God's people have been served by many prophets, but they belong to his Son.

Secondly, as God made the worlds through him, it is clear that both Father and Son were active in the creation of all things. Furthermore it is obvious that the Son existed before all things, for otherwise he could have had no part in creating them. Once God spoke through the prophets. These men were limited, like us, to a brief and fragile life, but now he reveals himself in the person of One who is eternal. Verse 3 tells us that the same Son upholds *all things by the word of his power*. This does not mean that Jesus is like Atlas in the Greek myths, supporting the weight of the planet on his shoulders. No, he actively controls the universe in order to accomplish his purposes. God's messenger created everything and rules over everything. He is God!

Verse 3 goes on to describe Jesus as *the brightness of his glory*. He is not bright with the glory of God; he is the very radiance itself. Sunbeams are inseparable from the sun. In the same way Jesus and his Father share the same essence. Because of Jesus sinful human beings may know what the invisible God is like. In John 1:18 we are told that Jesus, simply by being himself, has revealed the God who could never have been known otherwise. No prophet could ever declare the truth of God as completely as Jesus, for he is *God the only begotten* (NIV margin). The Son of God can reveal the Father to us because he shares his divine nature.

Verse 3 also calls him *the express image of His person*. That phrase 'express image' means something like a coin-maker's mould or stamp. The coin matches the mould exactly. The correspondence is complete. As the Father is, so is the Son.

They are not merely alike, they are identical in nature. Everything that is true of the Father is true of Jesus. Do you want to know what God is like? Do you want to understand his character and his ways? The prophets will teach you much that is valuable, but best of all, go to Jesus. Take a long, steady look at the Son of God. Read about him in the Word of God, listen to preaching that exalts him, pray to him, lean upon him, learn to love him and serve him. Let him be your teacher in the ways of God. No one else knows the subject as he does, and there is no other teacher like him.

Moreover, we learn here that the Son *purged* the sins of his people. Sin defiles. It makes people dirty. Their moral nature becomes tainted and unclean. Who can cleanse himself from the stains of a sinful past? There is no point in trying. It cannot be done. All the religions that encourage people to undertake some form of self-cleansing are futile. It is a hopeless task. Even the greatest of the prophets cannot help us here. All they can do is to point us in the direction of the one who can. For example, John the Baptist exclaimed when he saw Jesus coming towards him, *Look, the Lamb of God who takes away the sin of the world* (John 1:29). Cleansing is available but only the Son can provide it. If those Jewish Christians were to reject him, they would be saying goodbye to pardon and peace with God.

Where are the prophets now? They serve God in heaven. Where is the Son now? He is at *the right hand* of the Father, sharing the throne, ruling and reigning with him.

It was not the author's intention to belittle the prophets of old. God spoke through them. Judaism was a divinely ordained religion. Even so, it was in the process of being superseded by the same God who had first ordained it. He had something for the world that was far better. This shows the peril that the first readers of this epistle faced. They were contemplating leaving the greater thing behind in order to return to the lesser. What folly! What would they gain by it? Their rejection might bring an end to persecution, but they would be travelling back into the past, to a system that was only intended to be preparatory and which was rapidly becoming obsolete.

Conclusion

Why is Jesus greater than the prophets? A prophet is a mediator who is a man, and no more than a man. He is subject to all the limitations of his species. But now, *in these last days*, God has revealed himself through one who has no limitations at all because he is God. At the same time, the Son who reveals God to us is a man. God has come to us face to face. God has come to us as one of us. The Son brings us a final revelation of God. It is true, it is accurate, it is complete. As Jesus said, *he who has seen me has seen the Father* (John 14:9).

Jesus is God's final word to the human race. In saying this we are not being negative. Instead we put Jesus in his rightful place. God has nothing more to say to the world because Jesus represents him with complete accuracy. We need no more. Islam claims that it is a new revelation that supersedes Christianity. The Roman Catholic Church claims to be a prophet in its own right, with the power to reveal new truths. Are we not content with Jesus? Dare we say that in sending him to this world God has left something unsaid? We thank God for the prophets. We thank him again because their task is finished. The One of whom they spoke is among us, and having him we reject all who would take his place.

3
JESUS – HIS NAME IS HIGHER THAN ANY OTHER

Please read Hebrews 1:4-6

Introduction

One word that stands out in this epistle is the word 'better'. Christians have a better hope than other people. In particular, believers today enjoy a better hope than godly Israelites did before the coming of Christ. This is because it is based on better promises. Because of Jesus we come to God with a better sacrifice than those of ancient Israel. More than that: Jesus himself is better than any other mediator between God and man. We remind ourselves that this letter was written first of all to Jewish believers. They were being tempted to ask a vital question: Does it really make a difference? Does it matter if we go back to Judaism? If we give up Jesus are we really turning our backs on God? The same question often faces people today. Surely all that matters is that you have some sort of religion. Why insist that Islam, Buddhism and the others are all wrong? The epistle to the Hebrews tells us that there is no comparison. God could have sent no one better than his Son. We have already seen that Jesus is greater than the prophets. From v. 4 of ch.1 onwards the author invites us to consider Jesus in relation to the angels: *having become so much better than the angels, as He has by inheritance obtained a more excellent name than they.*

At first sight this seems strange. Nowadays no one would suggest that the Son of God was equal to the angels, or perhaps even subordinate to them, but in the first century there was a real temptation to think in that way. A significant group within Judaism at that time was the Essenes. Although the New Testament does not mention them they were as important as the Pharisees. (The famous Dead Sea scrolls are a library of sacred texts left behind by a monastic community of Essenes). These people thought highly of angels. For instance, they believed that at the end of time God would send two Messiah figures. A kingly Messiah would be subordinate to a priestly Messiah, and both would be under the authority of the archangel Michael. (The statement in 2:5 that God *has not put the world to come ... in subjection to angels* seems to be aimed at correcting this view.)

Let us not forget that the religion of Israel had one outstanding feature: the belief that God is one. *Hear, O Israel: The LORD our God, the LORD is one!* (Deuteronomy 6:4) No doubt these Jewish believers were being accused of denying this. Had they not made another God of this Jesus? A tempting way out would be to argue that calling someone the Son of God was not saying so much after all. Did not God himself refer to the angels as 'sons' of God? (Job 38:7 is a case in point). This epistle makes such ideas impossible. The Son whom God has sent into the world is a Son like no other. According to the first part of verse 5, Jesus takes the highest place: *For to which of the angels did He ever say: 'You are My Son, today I have begotten you'?* At this point the author directs our attention to the Old Testament. First century Hebrew Christians would be familiar with it, and would not take it lightly. His approach is straightforward. He makes a comparison. What does the Old Testament say about angels on the one hand, and about the Son of God on the other? His purpose was to prove that the early Christians actually understood the Old Testament better than the Jews did.

The claims that they made for Jesus were no more and no less than the claims that the Old Testament made about him before he came into the world. Altogether we have seven quotations in the first chapter of this letter. They are not chosen at random: each one builds on the rest. They mount up to a climax. The total picture leaves us in no doubt. Jesus has no rivals: his name is higher than any other. For the moment we will concentrate on the first three quotations from the Old Testament. These form a unit, and deal with the relationship between God and his Son.

Jesus: declared to be the Son of God

The first of our series of Old Testament passages is taken from Psalm. 2:7. We will understand this best if we try to grasp the message of the whole psalm. It may well be the case that this psalm was originally composed during a crisis in the history of Israel. One of her kings, perhaps even David himself, was in danger. His enemies had come together to plot his downfall. However the psalmist spoke of more than he knew. These words are not merely the words of an Israelite king facing a hostile confederacy. Messiah himself is speaking. Look at vv 1-2 of Psalm 2. *Why do the nations rage, and the people plot a vain thing? The kings of the earth set themselves, and the rulers take counsel together, against the LORD and against His Anointed.* Who is the anointed One? When did hostile rulers set themselves against the Lord's anointed? The first Christians were in no doubt. Turn to Acts 4: 24-27. This records the response of those first believers to the imprisonment of Peter and John. They quote this very psalm. As far as they were concerned it was a prophecy fulfilled at the cross.

Did Pilate, Herod and the chief priests realise what they were doing? They were not simply opposing a north-country prophet and teacher. If anyone sets himself against the Lord's anointed he sets himself against the Lord himself. As Psalm 2:4 shows, God holds defiance from such puny creatures in contempt. Who are the great ones of this world to oppose the Almighty? God's answer is to vindicate his Son. In Psalm 2:6, God speaks to a rebellious world in support of his Son, *Yet I have set My King On My holy hill of Zion* and in verse 7 Messiah speaks of the Lord's decree concerning him. *I will declare the decree: The LORD has said to Me, 'You are My Son, Today I have begotten You'.* The closing phrase in Psalm 2:7, *Today I have begotten You*, has worried some believers. Does it mean, as the Arians once argued and Jehovah's Witnesses still do, that there was once a time when the Son of God did not exist, that he had a beginning and is therefore somewhat less than wholly divine? We need to understand that the 'begetting' mentioned here is not a reference to the 'eternal begetting of the divine Son "before all worlds"'.[1] Instead, it refers to the begetting of the incarnate Son, not at Calvary but as the first example of a renewed humanity, the *firstborn among many brethren* (Romans 8:29). When did this happen? The apostle Paul has identified the moment for us. In his sermon at Antioch in Pisidia, he said, *And we declare to you glad tidings – that promise which was made to the fathers. God has fulfilled this for us their children, in that He has raised up Jesus. As it is also written in the second Psalm: 'You are My Son, Today I have begotten You.'* (Acts 13:32-33). Psalm 2:7 was fulfilled at the resurrection of Jesus, where he was *declared to be the Son of God with power* (Romans 1:4). In Colossians 1:8 we read that Jesus is *the beginning, the firstborn from the dead*. Indeed in Hebrews 1:6 he is called the 'firstborn' and where there is a firstborn, others follow in due course. At his resurrection Jesus was begotten from the dead, the first of many more to come, people born again by the power of God and placed 'in Christ'.

Psalm 2 is teaching that the entire world is in rebellion against God. Every human being is involved. As a race we have defied

God, and challenged him to do his worst. The psalm makes it clear that this is tragic folly. Not even the generals and the presidents have the resources to wage war on the Almighty. Look at Psalm 2:10-12. *Now therefore, be wise, O kings; Be instructed, you judges of the earth. Serve the* LORD *with fear, and rejoice with trembling. Kiss the Son, lest He be angry, and you perish in the way, when His wrath is kindled but a little. Blessed are all those who put their trust in him.* The only way to be sure of blessing is to surrender to the God whom we have offended. Messiah calls us to repent of a life of defiance against God. If we do repent and come to Christ, the whole situation changes. Now we are on the winning side – the side of the one whom even death could not subdue!

We are now in position to sum up so far. The Old Testament predicted that God would proclaim his anointed Son, and establish him in spite of all the opposition the world could muster. This has come true in the person of Jesus. His resurrection proves it. Not even the mightiest of the angels can claim this. Jesus is exalted above the greatest of them. He has no equal.

Jesus: a Son for ever

The second quotation from the Old Testament is found in the second part of verse 5: *I will be to Him a Father, and He shall be to me a Son.* This quotation comes from 2 Samuel 7:14, from the words of the prophet Nathan who told King David that one of his descendants would build a house for God's name and would receive the throne of an everlasting kingdom. It is worth observing that Old Testament prophecies are often fulfilled at more than one level. That is certainly true here, for while David's immediate heir Solomon built the first temple in Jerusalem, this did not exhaust the significance of the prophecy.

The Israelite monarchy eventually came to an end. Nevertheless the prophecy was still not completely fulfilled. Isaiah reaffirmed it. (See Isaiah 9: 6,7). A Son was promised who would rule on David's throne for ever. Clearly the original promise to David referred to the coming of Messiah.

At this stage the author to the Hebrews wanted his readers to see that Jesus was that promised One. Once again, they must see that the Old Testament points to the coming of Jesus. Those Hebrew believers were tempted to revert to Judaism. Did they imagine that they could do without the New Testament revelation of Jesus, yet cling to what God had said in the Old Testament? This cannot be done. The great central message of the Old Testament is that God was going to send his Son into the world as mediator between God and man. If you deny that Jesus is the Messiah, you deny the Old Testament as well as the New. The Jew who will not have Jesus as the Lord's anointed is refusing the message of his own sacred Scriptures.

The writer adds something to the picture here. We saw that God has proclaimed Jesus as his Son. Now we see that this will always be so. His Sonship is everlasting. That relationship will endure for ever. There will never be a time when he will not be the Son of God. He is the unique Son. No angel can be compared with him. This has tremendous consequences for the Christian. Believers are called sons of God, and indeed they are, but only because Jesus is their mediator. They are sons because he is a Son, but while Christ is the Son of God by nature, believers are sons of God by grace. As their older brother he has won their acceptance with God. God now sees them as people 'in Christ'. His Sonship is perpetual; so now their sonship is too. God looks upon every individual believer and says of him, 'I will be to him a Father, and he shall be to me a son.' Since Jesus will not cease to be the Son of God, his brothers shall not cease to be sons of God either. A Christian's place in God's love is permanent because Jesus' place in it is permanent.

Jesus: the Son whom all will acknowledge

The third quotation from the Old Testament is found in verse 6: *But when He again brings the firstborn into the world, He says: 'Let all the angels of God worship Him.'* This is taken from Deuteronomy 32:43, part of a section known as the song of Moses. It is not included in the text upon which the Authorised version and New King James Version are based, but it is found in the Dead Sea Scrolls, and the Septuagint (i.e. the Greek Old Testament that was available to the author). The Hebrew fragment from the Dead Sea Scrolls actually reads, 'Let all the sons of God worship him.'

Moreover, this phrase is also found in Psalm 97:7 where it reads, *Worship Him, all you gods.* We need to understand that Psalm 97 is one of a group of psalms that deal with the theme of God's judgement. We can see this in Psalm 96:13. *For He is coming, for He is coming to judge the earth. He shall judge the world with righteousness, and the peoples with His truth.* Psalm 98:9 repeats the thought. *For He is coming to judge the earth. With righteousness He shall judge the world, and the peoples with equity.* But when God comes to judge the world, what will be the manner of his coming? Look at Psalm 97:2–6. It will be a coming that every one shall see. It will bring calamity and ruin to the created world. This agrees with what the New Testament tells us about the second coming of Jesus. We can therefore be sure that Psalm 97 refers not merely to God, but to his Messiah. The One whom the angels worship is the One who is coming to judge the world. The New Testament confirms this (see Acts 17:31).

How great is Jesus! The day is coming when every living soul will see his greatness. The apostle Paul spells it out for us in Philippians 2: 9–11. *Therefore God ... has highly exalted Him and given Him the name which is above every name, that at the name of Jesus every knee should bow, of those in heaven, and of those on earth, and of those under the earth, and that every tongue should confess that Jesus Christ is Lord, to the glory of God the Father.* Angels and men alike will all admit that Jesus is Lord. Believers will admit it with joy and delight, others to their never-ending sorrow, but all will admit it! It will be as clear as day. The Son whom God has sent into the world is himself God. He has no rivals. No one can rank alongside him.

Summary of verses 4-6

Whether we are Christians or not, we cannot escape the force of this passage of Scripture. It is impossible to think too highly of Jesus. Those of us who are believers need to recapture this sense of his awesome grandeur. God has not sent us a prophet or a shining messenger from the world of the angels. The Lord of glory himself has come. The Christian faith does not offer the world a religious teacher much like the others who have come and gone over the centuries. Away with the gurus and the pundits, the false teachers of one kind or another! O Christian! *What is your beloved more than another beloved?* (Song of Solomon 5:9)   He is chief among ten thousand!

For those who are not Christians there is a solemn thought here. If a person rejects the teachings of Confucius or Aristotle they will be none the worse for it, but they cannot afford to neglect Jesus. He is the greatest person in the entire universe. He is the One who will judge all mankind at the end of time and fix everyone's destiny for eternity. The lesson from the angels is – worship him!

---

[1]   Philip Edgecumbe Hughes, *A Commentary on the Epistle to the Hebrews*, p.55. Hughes' discussion on pp.55-56 is extremely helpful.

4

JESUS – THE EVERLASTING KING

Please read Hebrews 1:7-14

Introduction

The rest of chapter 1 continues the argument begun in verse 4 that Jesus, the Son of God, is greater than the angels. We noted that one group among the Jews of the first century, the Essenes, taught that once this world has run its course, the archangel Michael would be given authority over the world to come. Even Messiah would be subordinate to him. They believed that there would be two Messiahs, one royal, the other priestly. Moreover, Jews could point to places in their Scriptures which spoke of angels as sons of God. Perhaps this meant that Jesus was no greater than the angels? The author wanted to show that this kind of thinking dishonoured Jesus. He is a Son like no other.

The author's point is that Jesus stands alone. He is altogether unique. This was particularly relevant to converted Jews. This epistle makes it all clear. The religion of the Old Testament was preparatory. Without Jesus it is like a gate without a house, an arch without a capstone. The Old Testament testifies of Christ. It was not that the first Christians were innovators, far from it, for they had seen that the Old Testament only makes complete sense when we read it from the perspective of the New. If those Hebrew believers were to be faithful to their ancient Scriptures, they would have to follow Jesus. This is why the author uses so many quotations from the Old Testament. In this section he selects seven. Together they show that Jesus is the promised Messiah of the Old Testament, and greater than the angels. As we have seen, the first three quotations prove that Jesus is indeed the unique Son of God. Now we look at the rest. We have learned that the Son of God reigns, but what will his kingdom be like?

An everlasting Kingdom

The fourth quotation from the Old Testament is found in verse 7: *And of the angels He says: 'Who makes His angels spirits and His ministers a flame of fire'*. This quotation is taken from Psalm 104:4. The author had the Greek Septuagint version of the Old Testament before him, which reads, 'He makes His angels winds.' (The word 'spirit' in the Authorised Version is probably used because the same Hebrew word can mean either wind or spirit). The angels are mighty beings. They are like forces of nature. God uses them as he uses the rushing wind or the bolt of lightning. They herald his presence and glory. Nevertheless, they are not independent. They have no authority to act on their own. They are God's servants. (That is the original sense of the word 'ministers' in verse7). Furthermore they are created servants. God 'makes' them. They are what they are because the Almighty fashioned them in that way.

The angels are limited, finite beings. It is not so in the case of the Son. The author draws a contrast. (Compare the opening words of v.7 with those of v.8). This brings us to the fifth passage from the Old Testament, which is found in verses 8 - 9:

But to the Son He says: 'Your throne, O God is for ever and ever; A sceptre of righteousness is the sceptre of Your Kingdom. You have loved righteousness and hated lawlessness; Therefore God, your God has anointed You with the oil of gladness more than your companions'.

This quotation is taken from Psalm 45:6-7. This wedding psalm was perhaps originally written to commemorate the marriage of one of the kings of Israel. If we look at verses 4-5 of the psalm it seems that the king in question was a warrior, a rugged and redoubtable conqueror who triumphed over his enemies. At the same time the writer says certain things of him which could never be said of any human monarch. No earthly king, the writer says, will sit upon his throne forever! This is because the psalm is Messianic. First of all it looks at the king in Jerusalem, but then it looks beyond him to the great King who is still to come. The latter part of the psalm (verse 10 onwards) speaks of the King's bride, and the glorious wedding day when Messiah takes his favoured spouse to be his own. We have here the wonderful prospect of that happy day when Christ and his church will be united for ever. Clearly the psalm tells us of a human king, but it addresses him as *God* (6). Therefore the king can only be that unique individual, Jesus Christ, who, though a man, was *declared to be the Son of God with power ... by the resurrection from the dead* (Romans 1:4). In passing, we should note that we have in verse 8 an explicit and unambiguous reference to Jesus as God. This is by no means the only reference of its kind in the New Testament. Several other Biblical authors make the same point. (See John 1:1; Romans 9:5; Titus 2:13; 2 Peter 1:1.) The fact that our King is divine helps us to deduce certain things about the Kingdom. It derives its character from the King! To begin with we see that it is an everlasting kingdom. Verse 8 speaks of a throne, which is *for-ever and ever*. Human kingdoms are not like that. Rulers grow old and die, dynasties crumble, and empires fade away. We read that each king of Israel died and was buried with his fathers. No one nowadays fears Napoleon or Nebuchadnezzar. The empire of Rome is an ancient story, and that of Britain a memory. Over the centuries many people have sacrificed their lives for causes that ultimately came to nothing.

No Christian will be disillusioned in that way. It is true that religious fashions come and go, churches rise and fall, and denominations sink into oblivion, but be confident of this: there will always be Christians. The gospel itself is a cause that will never become obsolete. It is not a movement whose time has passed. Believers are citizens of a kingdom that cannot end. The gospel will always be a force to reckon with. When ten thousand years of eternity are over, even then the kingdom of Messiah will have the brightest of futures ahead of it, and on its throne the man who is God will still reign in splendour.

The quotation from Psalm 45 also tells us that this will be a righteous kingdom. That is because the King is righteous! Who *loved righteousness and hated lawlessness* (9) more than the Lord Jesus? That statement sums up his ministry. Of all the people that ever lived he alone never once fell into sin. He has nothing against his record. He will never need to say 'sorry'. This should not surprise us. Everything about God is righteous. He can never compromise. His love is a holy love. God cannot love at the expense of his moral perfection. He bore the consequences of his holy wrath against sin in the person of his Son, Jesus. Verse 9 shows that a righteous Father loves the righteousness of the Son. *The oil of gladness* refers to the Holy Spirit who was poured out on the Son as a result of his obedience.

In a righteous kingdom the unrighteous have no place. Since we have no righteousness of our own it is vital that we receive the righteousness of Christ. Unless we are made right with God there will be no place for us in his holy kingdom. Are we already servants of his? Then we must be holy. Subjects of a holy King must share the royal attitude to sin and righteousness. If we do not, we deny that he is King over us.

An everlasting King

Verses 10–12 give us the sixth quotation from the Old Testament:

> And 'You, LORD, in the beginning laid the foundation of
> the earth, And the heavens are the work of Your hands;
> They will perish, but You remain; And they will all grow
> old like a garment; Like a cloak You will fold them up,
> And they will be changed. But You are the same and
> Your years will not fail,

These verses quote Psalm 102: 25–27. This psalm is the prayer of a believer grieving over the low state of Zion. Zion was another name for the city of Jerusalem, but it also represents the cause of God on this earth. At first the Psalmist mourns because God appears to have neglected his cause, but increasingly he comes to a quiet trust in a never-failing God. The last few verses of the psalm are especially important. Once again we see the longer perspective. Look at vv 23-24a. *He weakened my strength in the way; He shortened my days. I said, 'O my God, Do not take me away in the midst of my days'.* It is Messiah who speaks, pleading that he should not be cut off. At this point we leap across the centuries and anticipate the evening in Gethsemane when the Son of God asked if the cup of suffering could be taken from him. Verses 24b–27 are the Lord's answer, his words of reassurance to Messiah. *Your years are throughout all generations. Of old You laid the foundation of the earth, And the heavens are the work of Your hands. They will perish, but You will endure; Yes, they will all grow old like a garment; Like a cloak You will change them, And they will be changed. But You are the same, And Your years will have no end.* Something similar is recorded in John 12: 27-28. As God the Son confronted the dreadful outcome of his mission, God

the Father came to him with words that strengthened him to meet the great yet terrible climax of his mission. *Now My soul is troubled, and what shall I say? 'Father, save Me from this hour'? But for this purpose I came to this hour.*
'Father, glorify Your name.' Then a voice came from heaven, saying, 'I have both glorified it and will glorify it again.'

Messiah cannot be extinguished. Even death will not be the end of him. This is because he is the Creator of all things. He is not merely greater than the angels, he is greater than everything, for he made everything. He made Palestine, Herod, Pilate, and the tree on which he was crucified. The men who killed him were all his creatures. The animals and people who live upon the face of the earth are subject to the forces of nature, but not the one who created the whole universe. When it all ends he will still be there. 'In the beginning' he was active in bringing it all into being. In the end it will all cease to be because of his power. God's word to Messiah is that his trials will have a glorious outcome. When the present order of things has ended, he will remain.

We tend to think of the earth as something durable and permanent. In comparison with the natural world we ourselves only live a short time. Yet although the universe has lasted far longer than we have, there is nothing permanent about it. Even scientists who are not Christians acknowledge that the universe will not go on forever. Will it all end in the distant future, when the sun loses its heat? Will global warming finish us off some time next century? Perhaps insecure politicians will destroy the world in a nuclear cataclysm. The perspective of this epistle is that the Son of God is in control. As a man wraps up his cloak, the everlasting Son will close the story of the ages. There is a tragedy at the heart of much human endeavour. People plan and sacrifice, toil and build, all for a system which is certainly to perish. How sad it is! All that effort, and none of it will last.

Only one thing never changes. It is said of Messiah, *You are the same, and your years will not fail.* The kingdom is everlasting because the King is everlasting. All around us things change. This often brings disappointment. The things that seemed so secure let you down in the end. But the Christian has no cause for dismay. High above the turmoil and decay there is the unchanging King, secure in his control of all things. He is not fickle and unpredictable. He has no moods. Nothing about him ever alters. He will never cease to be righteous, and he will never stop loving his own with an unconquerable, irresistible love. A person who longs for permanence and stability will only find them in Jesus.

However, are we not part of this doomed system? Are we not flesh and blood, part of the creation? Look again: who is it that reigns for ever? A man occupies the eternal throne. God gives these promises of everlasting dominion to One who took our humanity, and who wears it in heaven for us. Psalm 102 concludes with verse 28 in this way; *The children of Your servants will continue, and their descendants will be established before You.* Messiah will continue, and so will his servants. Because the King reigns for ever, his subjects will serve him for ever. He will never cease to be our Father; we will never cease to be his children.

Now, in the meantime

The seventh quotation from the Old Testament, occurs in verse 13:

> But to which of the angels has he ever said: 'Sit at my right hand, till I make Your enemies Your footstool'. Are they not ministering spirits sent forth to minister for those who will inherit salvation?

This quotation is taken from Psalm 110:1. This too is a messianic psalm. Jesus himself quoted from it in Matthew 22:41-46 to correct the Pharisees mistaken ideas about the Messiah. It opens with the words, *The LORD said to my* (David's) *Lord.* Again we have an instance of communication between the Almighty and his anointed. Messiah is invited to take the highest place of all. The angels stand before God. They are 'ministering spirits' sent to and fro to serve the interests of believers (14). The Son, by contrast, is seated. The place of honour is his. However let us observe that he is invited to take his seat. He has not always occupied it. He has, until now, been about his Father's business. His incarnation, his life of service, his death for sinners have taken place, and now that he is risen and ascended he is exalted to the highest place.

Nevertheless this is not the end. Something is yet to come. His enemies have not yet been made his footstool. In the East victorious generals placed their feet on the necks of defeated enemies to show that their conquest was complete. We need this reminder. We must keep patience and not lose heart. As we see it the world is in a mess. Christian! Nothing has gone wrong. All is as it should be. The psalm predicted it and Hebrews confirms it. Once Messiah had returned to his glory and was seated with his Father, there was to be a pause. We live in a transitional period, in between the ages, 'in these last days'. The age of Messiah is imminent, but not yet. In the meantime God gathers in his elect, completing his church. Soon, no one can tell just how soon, this age of change and decay will end. The King himself is preparing an everlasting Kingdom.

Summary of verses 7-14

There is no doubt that the New Testament has much to say about the glory and the uniqueness of Christ. Even so, this wonderful theme does not occur only in the New Testament and nowhere else. The first people to read this epistle were Christians of Jewish extraction. They needed to be reminded that the Scriptures that they had grown up with, our Old Testament, should have prepared them for all that the New Testament said about Jesus. If they chose to reject the message of the New Testament they could not pass this off as a return to the religion of their childhood and their ancestors. Reject what the New Testament says about Christ and you reject the message of the Old Testament along with it. The Bible is one book with a single message and that message is Christ in all his greatness, the ruler of an unshakeable kingdom whose permanence is guaranteed because he himself will endure forever. Christians can therefore face the challenges posed by a hostile world with calm strength. For all the difficulties we face in the here and now our future inheritance is certain because the Christ who has promised it cannot change.

5
A SOLEMN WARNING

Please read Hebrews 2:1-4

Introduction

This short section of the epistle takes advantage of a new stage in the argument. The author has been explaining that Jesus, the Son of God, is greater than the angels. In chapter 1 he showed that the Son is divine. None of the angels occupies an everlasting throne exalted above the entire creation! As we shall see, in chapter 2, the author goes on to say that the Son is also greater than the angels are because he is human. They cannot mediate between God and men, for they are quite unable to represent human beings. By contrast, the mediator, who is himself a man, can do so. At this point (1–4) the author pauses before going on to deal with this aspect of the Son's humanity. All along his thrust has been that God is now speaking to mankind through his Son. We ignore this message at our peril. According to these four verses, those who do not give heed to God's Son will not escape the consequences.

How much is at stake? (1)

Everything is at stake. Those first century Hebrew Christians were in danger of drifting away (1). Picture a boat in a calm estuary. It lies up against the jetty. It seems safe enough, but is not anchored. When the tide ebbs away, or a storm blows up, the boat will be lost, and all because it was never tied up securely in the first place. The author challenges his original readers to look to their spiritual moorings. They had God's revelation of his truth, but this by itself would never suffice. When the pressure came on, and the storms of persecution arose, would they prove to be firmly anchored, or would they drift? This warning note is one of the most obvious features of the book. (Look at 3:12,13 and 10:28 – 31). Here were people who had attended Christian meetings, were accepted by the community of believers, but were never truly secure, and once their position was exposed they lost everything.

Nothing has changed. This passage is a warning to the person who has heard what God has to say, and so far has not responded. Is it really so bad to close one's ears to God? Is it really such a sin to sit in church irritated and bored by it all? Perhaps it would not matter so much if we only refused to take much notice of the preacher, but have you considered that through the preacher God offers a great salvation? Look at the generosity of it. Jesus stands with arms stretched wide to receive all who will come to him. He says that he will never turn them away. He guarantees rest for the troubled conscience, forgiveness for the vilest of sins, and pleads with the uncaring and hard-hearted to be at peace with God. The man who gathered wood at Sinai died for despising God, and the man who closes his mind to the gospel despises Christ and will not escape his judgement.

A longstanding principle (2)

We need to be clear what the author had in mind when he wrote about the *word spoken through angels* (2). This is a reference to the law, given at Mount Sinai. It is easy to assume that when God gave the law, he was alone with Moses. This was not so. In Deuteronomy 33:2 Moses himself said that with God were *ten thousands of saints* (i.e. holy ones). In the same way, Stephen referred to the law as having been given by angels (Acts 7:38, 53), as did the apostle Paul (Galatians 3:19). Nevertheless, though the angels acted as intermediaries, the message that was given to Moses came from God himself. The law was a gracious revelation of his holiness. Sadly it was not long before someone broke the law. Keeping the Sabbath was one of the commandments. That day was set apart from the other days of the week, a day not for work but for worship. Numbers 15: 32–36 records an incident where a man was caught gathering sticks on the Sabbath. He was placed in custody until Moses could find out what God wanted to be done. The verdict was that the man had to be stoned to death. This is what verse 2 is talking about when it mentions *transgression and disobedience* receiving the appropriate reward.

Many modern people react to this sort of thing with horror. Surely the offence was trivial, almost nothing! Why should the Almighty pick a quarrel with someone over a small amount of firewood? The same people, no doubt, feel that eating a piece of fruit is not important either, and that God treated Adam and Eve with a severity out of all proportion to the offence. We must never allow ourselves to think like this. Nothing that God commands can ever be trivial. The sin was serious, not because of the action itself, but because it was committed against a great person. Roman Catholicism teaches that some sins are 'venial', so insignificant that they are hardly worthy of notice. Let there be no doubt about it: there are no trifling sins. Every sin is an attempt to tell God that his requirements do not matter, that we can pick and choose between them and decide which we will observe, and which do not suit us. We imply that created beings can treat the one who created them with contempt, and that servants can obey their Master only when it suits them. The important thing about the man who gathered sticks was his defiant and rebellious attitude to God. ('Never mind what he thinks...'). The punishment that he received was no more than he deserved. God always deals like this with human beings since his justice never varies. Those who offend against his majesty and holiness will not escape. They did not do so when God spoke through angels, nor will they do so now, when he speaks through his Son.

God's new revelation brings greater urgency (3)

We cannot argue that God has not taken mankind seriously. For God to communicate with human beings at all is remarkable. Now consider that he no longer contents himself with speaking through prophets or angels. These no longer suffice. He entrusted the gospel of reconciliation to the greatest of messengers. As verse 3 tells us, God the Son spoke the message of salvation. God did not merely send someone, he came himself in the person of his Son. If God deserves our attention when an angel brings the message, he deserves it all the more when his own Son delivers it.

So great a salvation (3-4)

The most tragic people on earth are those who neglect God. Consider what they miss by it. Verse 3 speaks of a *great salvation*, and so it is. The author chose to stress this because his readers were tempted to believe otherwise. The propaganda of the Jewish authorities was that Christianity was beneath contempt. Its founder was a condemned criminal who had been executed with the most degrading penalty that Roman law could inflict. Jesus was a disgraced and discredited man. The whole thing was scandalous. Christians facing the challenges of a world that is very different can find that a similar attitude still exists today. If you talk about salvation people think of you as a quaint extremist. Religion, they tell us, is about morals, ceremony, and the great social problems of the age! If you say that religion has something to do with being saved you will be an object of ridicule. There is an attitude that says that only cultists, 'fundamentalists' and eccentric people think like that. 'Oh, you've been saved, have you? You're one of them!' The salvation described in Hebrews 2 is neither an object for scorn nor pity. It is not contemptible. It is the grace of God in action; it is a great salvation. The very angels of God wonder at the greatness of it and ponder its riches.

Those who have been saved cannot see it any other way. It is a great salvation because of the plight that they were in. The rescue of a sinner is no trivial thing. As human beings we are law-breakers who have offended God. We are condemned criminals awaiting execution, and the sentence that awaits us is no less than eternal death. The gospel is good news of the most exuberant kind. God does not merely change our sentence and give us a lesser penalty – He gives us a pardon that is absolute and complete. Do not tell a man who knows conviction of sin, who feels the weight of his guilt before God, that this salvation is a mere notion. Christians are people who have been lifted, in a moment, from the lowest depths to the greatest heights imaginable. What a transfer! From the brink of eternal ruin to glory, and to the status of brotherhood with Christ (see verse 11).

Another reason why we can describe this as a great salvation is that a great Saviour has accomplished it. The remainder of chapter 2 elaborates this idea. The only person who could bring *many sons to glory* (10) was the mediator himself. He had all the resources of God at his command, for he himself is God. The Saviour had to confront sin, temptation, Satan and even death. No one but God could encounter each of these foes and triumph over them. At the same time this salvation required a mediator who could identify in every way with those whom he came to save, one who was as human as they are. In the whole vast universe there is only one individual with the necessary combination of qualities. Our Saviour is the everlasting God who was made, during the time of his life on earth, *a little lower than the angels* (7). If we were able to assemble all the angels and every human person together it would be as clear as day. There is no one like Jesus.

Furthermore this is a great salvation because it takes sin seriously. Some religions think lightly of sin, and suppose that the good that we do outweighs the evil. Some argue that God could have saved us simply by exercising his power, plucking sinners out of hell and into heaven without changing them. God, however, is always faithful to his character. He never loves at the expense of his holiness. He punishes, with the utmost rigour, the sin that has offended his holy nature, but it is not the sinner who suffers the punishment. Verse 9 tells us that Jesus tasted death *for everyone*. There is some debate as to whether this is the best way to translate the Greek. Some scholars favour the idea that it ought to read 'for everything' as though the author was emphasising the fact that the redemption Christ has purchased will effect not only his people but the whole of creation. It is better, however, to stay with the traditional rendering. In v.6 the author asks the question, *what is man?* And in v.10 he writes of Jesus *bringing many sons to glory* by his sufferings. The author has people, not creation at large, in view. The grace of God has fallen mankind as its object. It was for sinful humanity that Christ tasted death for his people. Their sin is punished, the debt is paid, the accounts are cleared, and all at His expense.

The sheer wonder of it only increases the urgency of our situation. When God pleads with people to be reconciled to him this is no small matter. He calls us to respond to the most wonderful invitation that anyone has ever made. The clear implication of this passage is that there are people who neglect this great salvation, and who do not escape. Do they know what they are refusing?

Few things prove the truth of human sinfulness more than the hostility that Jesus received. Surely if anyone ever deserved a hearing it was he. Here was a uniquely gifted communicator, a teacher like no other. Here was the only man in history whose life was a perfect advertisement for his message. Nothing in his character detracted from his teaching. Also, God corroborated Jesus' teaching in the most amazing way. Verse 4 tells us about the *signs and wonders, with various miracles* that accompanied the ministry of Jesus, and indeed of the apostles. The Hebrew believers had to pause at this point. They were wondering whether they could safely deny their profession of faith in Christ. To be a conscientious Jew would be enough to satisfy God, would it not? The author replies that God has spoken in Christ, and those who ignore what God says have never prospered. We too must *give the more earnest heed* (1). If we hear what he says to us in Christ, and then do nothing about it, we drift away from God.

Summary of Verses 1–4

The compassion of Christ underlies everything that we have considered in this passage. Jesus came to seek and save the lost. This is why he died and ever since that time he has not stopped caring, for through his servants he calls upon the people of our time to be reconciled to him. If someone is to perish forever it must mean that they have committed a sin that is truly monstrous. This is certainly the case. Few sins are worse than knowing that God has spoken yet ignoring him. Such people know perfectly well who they refuse, and what they refuse. It is agonising to say it, but they will not escape. We cannot mock God. He will not be gracious forever in the face of blatant rudeness. Do not play with God's offer of mercy. If you know that God has invited you to come to him, then do as he says. To respond in any other way is to risk losing everything.

6
JESUS – MADE LOWER THAN THE ANGELS

Please read Hebrews 2:5-18

Introduction

Verse 5 of this chapter is a link between what has gone before and what is to follow. This reminds us of the argument in chapter 1 that Jesus, the Son of God, is greater than the angels. Some first century Jews, the Essenes, believed that the archangel Michael would have a special role in the events at the end of history. Two Messianic figures would emerge, one a priest, the other a King, and both would be under his authority. *The world to come*, however, will not *be in subjection to angels*, for there is one who is greater than they are. His greatness lies in the fact that he is God, the unchanging one, whose years will not fail. This is not the whole of it. Chapter 2 brings us another aspect of the Son's greatness. He was *made a little lower than the angels* (9). Truly, he is great because he is divine, but he is also great because he shares our humanity.

The truth about mankind

Once again, the author of the epistle takes us back into the Old Testament. In verses 6-8 we have a quotation from Psalm 8:4-6. This psalm exalts the greatness of God in creation, and reminds us of much that is said in the book of Genesis. All that God made is a reminder of his glory and power, and the climax of it all is the human race (Psalm 8:3). Compared with the heavens, the moon and stars, what is man that God should concern himself about him? Indeed God has done more than simply take notice of humanity. He has given man dominion over the rest of creation. Of all created things, human beings are the most exalted. God has appointed them to be the under-stewards of the natural order.

There is something tragic about mankind. We all share in this tragedy simply because we are human. These verses explain the nature of this tragedy. Because of their sin and rebellion against God human beings must die. In this respect they are now placed below the never-dying angels. (This state of things is only temporary; the Greek tells us that man is lower than the angels 'for a little while'. Mortality will not always be an essential component of humanity). Also, as verse 8 says, *we do not yet see all things put under Him*. Man was made in the image of God, but that image is now spoiled because of sin. In consequence man is a sad sight. The irony is that though he was meant to exercise lordship over the natural order, he is all too often at the mercy of it. This is because he is not in control of himself. So often he uses his human ingenuity to harm the natural world. The power of the human mind is often used in destructive ways. Even then, man is by no means in control. He is humbled by the awesome power of the elements, and reduced to helplessness by forces that he cannot master.

At the same time, this psalm does not merely concern itself with man in general. It also looks forward to one man in particular. Verse 9 tells us that we see Jesus. He too was made lower than the angels, and all things have been placed under his authority. We do not yet see this as it has not been revealed to the world. Reflect for a moment. Mortality is a curse. Human beings die because they sin. However, if they had been like the angels they would never have borne children. Here we see the grace and wisdom of God, for although men and women must die, they do have descendants, and this made it possible in the purposes of God for a descendant of Adam and Eve to remedy the ancient curse. The Saviour of mankind is himself a man.

Jesus: a man who is not ashamed of his fellows

The Jewish Christians who received this epistle had to face the taunts of their Hebrew relatives and friends. Jesus had suffered death (9). The very idea that he could be Lord was preposterous! He was a failure, a loser, and a man whom God had rejected. It was tempting for the first readers of this epistle to feel ashamed of him and to ask themselves whether God could have achieved his purposes in some other way. Was crucifixion really necessary? Was there no alternative? It was degrading and shameful! The author wanted to reassure his readers. Verse 9 indicates that two momentous things depended upon the cross. First of all, Jesus had to *taste death* in order to enter into his glory. His exaltation is as high as it is because he willingly submitted himself to the *death of the cross* (see Philippians 2:5-11). Furthermore the salvation of sinners depended on it. His death was not like ours. He did not pay the penalty for his own wrongdoing as we do. He tasted death for others.

Verse 10 amplifies this. It gives us a glimpse into the mind of the God who made everything, and for whom everything exists. This verse tells us that God's intention was to bring *many sons to glory*. This could only be achieved in one way. The pioneer of their salvation, the one who made it all possible and brought it about, had to suffer. For him, it was the road he must travel to reach the perfection of his present glory. For us, it was absolutely vital. No Christian should feel ashamed of Jesus. His sufferings were *fitting*. They were an absolute moral and spiritual necessity.

Verse 11 says that Jesus sanctifies his people, that is, he makes them holy, acceptable to God. Moreover, the Holy One himself (*he who sanctifies*) and the people that he makes holy (*those who are being sanctified*) are *all of one*. He and they are brothers. Verse 12 illustrates this by quoting from Psalm 22. This psalm is divided into two parts, each one dealing with the experience of Messiah. In the first part David, speaking as a prophet, portrays in graphic detail the suffering of the Saviour. (Jesus, himself, quoted from the psalm: Matt. 27:46). In the second section, which begins in v.21, there is a distinct change of mood. It takes us beyond the suffering and agony. God has answered and vindicated his servant. *Save Me from the lion's mouth and from the horns of the wild oxen! You have answered Me. I will declare Your name to My brethren; In the midst of the assembly I will praise You.* (Psalm 22:21-22). This predicts clearly that once his sufferings were over the anointed servant of God would share his triumph with his brothers.

Verse 13 makes the same point. This time the Old Testament quotation is from Isaiah 8:17-18. It quotes the words of Isaiah himself. The kingdom of Judah was threatened by a coalition of enemies. The prophet could easily have become discouraged for the people were not responding to his warnings. Even so, Isaiah took heart. He had two children, and God had told him how to name each one. The name of the first, Maher-shalal-hash-baz (8:15), warned of judgement. (It means, 'He is hastening upon his prey'). In other words, just as a predator strikes like lightning, God would act decisively in punishing his guilty people). The name of the other, Shear-jashub (7:3), spoke of mercy. (It means 'a remnant shall return'). Even though God was justly angry with his people, he would not obliterate them completely but would spare a remnant. The names of Isaiah's two children make an important point about the character of God. We will never understand the Almighty unless we appreciate that holiness and mercy are both present in his nature and deserve equal emphasis. Isaiah's own name means 'Jehovah is salvation'. Now in Hebrews 2:13 the author puts Isaiah's words into the mouth of Messiah. ('Jesus' also means Jehovah is salvation.) He is not alone! God has given him children. He has a people. It all points ahead to the morning of the resurrection, and Jesus' words to the women: *Go and tell My brethren* (Matthew 28:10).

Suppose for a moment that God had appointed an angel as mediator between God and man. This would have been quite inappropriate. How can a spirit represent creatures of flesh and blood? Jesus, however, is all that we need. Here is no alien, but one who shares our nature. He is one with us, and in coming to our rescue he comes to help his own. As far as he is concerned there is complete solidarity. He is not aloof or detached from us. His attitude is that we are family, and even though we at times are ashamed to own up to our belonging to him, he is not ashamed to admit before a hostile world that we are his brothers.

What flesh and blood has accomplished

This chapter is a plea to take the humanity of Christ seriously. All the achievements of Christ were the achievements of a man, and in him, flesh and blood have done things that no angel could do. Look at v.16. The angels are not the objects of his love. The Son of God did not come into the world to rescue them. His interest was in human beings, the *seed of Abraham*. He saw them as his *children* (14).

The closing verses of this chapter leave us in no doubt that they needed his help. Their plight was terrible. Verse 15 describes one of the saddest features of the human condition: a lifetime lived under a cloud, the *fear of death*. This is a form of bondage that we cannot shake off. It might leave us for a

time, but it always returns. Satan exercises tyranny over us, reminding us of our certain end. We know that it will come, but
we do not know when. As human beings we deserve to die,
because of our sin. Verse 17 shows that the people whom Jesus
came to help had sins against their record. They would have to
encounter an angry God. He could only be propitiated, that is
his wrath could only be turned away, if a worthy offering could
be provided to placate his sense of offended justice. Who could
make such an offering? Only a priest who was not disqualified
by sin from drawing near to God.

The word *propitiation* in verse 17 is extremely important. It
is a word that describes the removal of wrath, in this case the
wrath of God against human sin, by the offering of a gift, in this
case, the self offering of Christ who is both priest and sacrifice.
On the one hand, *propitiation* reminds us that *God is light and
in Him is no darkness at all* (1 John 1:5). He is resolutely and
implacably opposed to evil in all its forms. Although he is *long-
suffering and abundant in mercy*, he *by no means clears the
guilty* (Numbers 14:18). On the other hand, *propitiation* also
includes the glorious and liberating fact that in Christ the holy
anger of God against sin can be put aside. At this point we
must take care to avoid a frequent misunderstanding. It is sometimes suggested that God the Father needed to be brought
round, much as an ill-tempered parent might be talked out of a
bad mood and that by offering himself as a sacrifice for sin,
Jesus pacified his Father. In actual fact, the initiative behind
propitiation rests with God the Father himself. Sinners are *justified freely by His grace through the redemption that is in Christ
Jesus* (Romans 3:24) because God set him forth *to be a propitiation by His blood, through faith, to demonstrate His righteousness* (Romans 3:25). The same God whose wrath *is
revealed from heaven against all ungodliness and
unrighteousness of men* (Romans 1:18) has responded in love
to the desperate plight of those whose sin has so grievously

offended him. *In this is love, not that we loved God, but that He loved us and sent His Son to be the propitiation for our sins* (1 John 4:10). Furthermore, in sending his Son, God did not send someone else to bear the enormous load of human guilt. Since Christ is God, it follows that in sending Jesus into our world, God came himself. At Calvary, the wrath of God against human sin was poured out in full. The claims of divine justice have been met and the one who bore the penalty is God himself, in the person of his Son. The wrath of God against sin and his love of sinners find their highest expression in the *propitiation* that Christ has made for the sins of his people.

Finally verse 18 tells us that human beings easily fall into temptation. We know this only too well. It tugs at us with a power that we are unable to withstand. What a mess the human race is in: weak, guilty and doomed to die.

Why is the gospel good news? It is because help is at hand, the best possible help. No angel could represent human beings *in things pertaining to God* (17). That is why the Son of God shared our nature (14). He was made like his brethren *in all things* (17). He was altogether human, fully human. He was as much a man as anyone alive today. He shared our humanity in every respect. He had all the qualities that belonged to man and woman. He had the body of a man; he was hungry, tired and so on. He had human emotions and a human soul, but unlike us he did not sin. (Sin, of course, is not a necessary part of human nature. It is an intruder.)

Here is something truly wonderful. Even though human flesh and blood has offended God and disgraced itself, God's grace is such that human flesh and blood comes to the rescue. A man has destroyed the power of Satan! A man has set free the captives of the devil! No believer need live in fear of death because a man has taken the terror from the grave. We can approach God with confidence. A man has taken away God's wrath. (Incidentally, let us not forget that this was the purpose

of God all along. We must not think that God the Father is
against us while God the Son is for us. God does not act against
himself!) When we confront temptation we can do so with
renewed confidence. A fellow man has met the same temptation at every point, and emerged from the trial victorious. He
knows how it feels to be probed and tested. We are not on our
own. How gracious God has been. Humanity failed at every
point yet though we are members of a beaten and humiliated
race we can be triumphant, for one of our own has won the
triumph.

We have a champion, one who has restored the whole situation, and set it all to rights. Glory to his great and worthy
Name! What a conqueror, what a victor! He is worthy of all the
admiration we can give. The victory was won at the cross. The
Hebrew Christians who first read this epistle were tempted to
give way under the pressure of their fellow Jews and agree that
the cross was a stumbling-block. It was offensive, something to
repudiate. Shame on the Christian who would ever repudiate
the cross of Christ! We only escape spiritual death because he
died. The one offering that would satisfy a righteous God was
the offering of his righteous life. The fact that he endured temptation is the one thing that guarantees our victory over it. If
Jesus had come to the world but not suffered at Calvary, we
would have been no better for it. He would have left commandments that we could not keep, an example we could not
follow, and made no atonement for our guilt. Is a dying
Saviour a reproach and an insult? No! The man who was
crucified will be the glory of the church and the wonder of the
ages.

7
JESUS – GREATER THAN MOSES

Please read Hebrews 3:1-6

Introduction (1)

Do people laugh at you because you are a Christian? Does the Christian life seem full of disadvantages? Do you sense that it is not worthwhile to follow Jesus? The epistle to the Hebrews was written to people who were discouraged. That is why this chapter opens as it does. It is no ordinary thing to be a Christian. Look at verse 1. Christians are brothers. At first sight this may not seem all that remarkable. It is quite common for people who belong to the same organisation to refer to each other as 'brothers'. Army officers speak about their 'brother officers' and Trade Unionists speak of their 'brothers' in the Labour movement. Christian brotherhood however, involves much more than affection and comradeship. We read in 2:11 that Jesus regards believers as his brothers. He sees no shame in that. He and his followers are one. They share human nature and eventually they will share the same character. Jesus is holy, and he is determined that his brothers should be holy too. Christians are remarkable people!

The world does not understand Christians. Things that interest ordinary people have little effect on them. They have a *heavenly calling*. Have you seen those ultra-high frequency whistles which dog-owners use? The dog hears a summons that no one else can detect. The believer is just the same. A voice from heaven has spoken and he must obey the call. The world looks on and wonders. Why is this person so different? Why does he not respond to the influences that sway everyone else? What drives him?

The author of the epistle tells his readers to *consider* Jesus. He calls men and women to follow him. When the pull of the old way of life threatens to draw believers back to things they have given up, the antidote is to consider Jesus. If they look at the Son of God everything else will seem unimportant by comparison. The glory of the Christian religion does not lie in its long list of heroes and martyrs, its heritage, its numbers of adherents or its places of worship. We elevate none of these things. What counts is Jesus! He is our 'Apostle', sent to be our great High Priest. Christians are only remarkable because they have a remarkable Saviour. Already we have seen that he is greater than both prophets and angels; now let us consider Jesus in comparison with Moses. First century Judaism had a galaxy of heroes. Great kings and prophets fill the pages of the Old Testament. Moses, however, makes them all look like dwarves. The first readers of this letter revered that great man. No doubt their Jewish neighbours sometimes reproved them. Had they not abandoned the great Moses for an impostor? As if to answer such charges the author takes nothing away from the giant of the exodus. However, when every tribute has been paid to his memory, a greater figure than Moses has emerged. People tell us today that there is not much difference between the great religious leaders of the past. Depend upon it! Jesus outshines them all.

A similarity (2)

In one respect Jesus and Moses were alike. Verse 2 tells us that both were faithful. Moses was a faithful servant of God. His record is impressive. In the name of the Lord he defied the despotic Pharaoh. Lesser men might have failed, but Moses carried out his commission to the letter. After leading the Israelites out of Egypt he led the people of Israel through the wilderness of Sinai for forty years. In the meantime, they contested his leadership at every step. He gave a lifetime of service for the infant nation of Israel, yet received no gratitude or reward. Few of the people appreciated the greatness of God, and few shared Moses' confidence in him. They were stubborn and refractory. Again and again they questioned his motives and misinterpreted everything he did. In the face of such a quarrelsome and unappreciative people Moses' consistency is almost incredible. In situations that would have provoked many gifted and experienced leaders beyond endurance, Moses stuck to his task. Even when others snapped, Moses did not give in to rage and petulance, but prayed for God's forgiveness for his exasperating people. Verse 2 alludes to an incident recorded in Numbers 12. Moses had married an Ethiopian woman. Miriam and Aaron, both of whom were normally reliable and loyal, were displeased, but God's verdict on his servant was that he was the meekest man on the face of the earth (see Numbers 12:1-8).

The life and ministry of Jesus show the same perseverance. Observe him in the Gospels and the same unflinching devotion to his task is clear. He faced obstacle after obstacle, and remained undaunted. His early preaching in his native Galilee met with suspicion and hostility. He was a prophet without honour in his own country. People accused him of the most offensive things — some even claimed that he was in league with the devil. His own followers were unpromising. Who would not have been driven to despair by such a collection of self-willed and fractious individuals? Moses at least had a Joshua and a Caleb! When Jesus needed support from his friends they could not give it, and he had to face the crisis of Calvary alone and unaided. Nevertheless, nothing could deflect him.

He steadfastly set His face to go to Jerusalem (Luke 9:51).
Reviewing his ministry he could say without exaggeration: *He
who sent me is with me. The Father has not left me alone, for I
always do those things that please Him* (John 8:29). Even the
certain knowledge that a violent and humiliating death awaited
him did not deflect him from the path of obedience.

However, we must not only note the similarity between Moses
and Jesus. Moses' record, outstanding as it is, was not perfect.
The complaints of the people eventually proved too much. The
Israelites had reached the wilderness of Kadesh, and demanded
water. God told Moses to strike the rock with his staff. He did
more than he was told to do and snapped in fury, *Hear now,
you rebels! Must we bring water for you out of this rock?*
(Numbers 20:10). By human standards Moses was a very
consistent leader. Jesus surpassed him. His record was one of
unending success. He achieved all his purposes. He never had
to confess failure. Many of us would be more than willing to
trust a man like Moses. Let us remember that there is only one
leader in the entire world without a failure to his name. Consider Jesus. Here is someone you can rely on. Entrust yourself
to his mercy and you can be sure of the outcome. He has never
broken a promise, never disappointed his millions of followers.
If you call upon him for mercy, will he really forgive you? If you
entrust yourself to him, will he protect you, keep you, and see
you safely through the wilderness of this world? Jesus is worthy
of your consideration. No one is as faithful as he is.

An important difference (3)

Moses and Jesus, we are told, were faithful in the service of
God's *house* (2). Obviously this was not a construction made
of bricks and mortar, but something intangible. British people
speak of the Royal House of Windsor, and this is a helpful way
to understand it. God's house is not a church building, but his

people. In Old Testament days it was primarily the nation of Israel, but now it is the Christian church, the whole family of converted people. Some are already in heaven and others are still on earth. Moses, himself head and shoulders above other great servants of God, was no more than a member of this house. He was not simply over the people of God; he was one of them. He illustrates the paradox of all spiritual leadership in the church of Christ. Every shepherd is also a sheep, with a sheep's ability to wander. Every preacher of righteousness is also a sinner. No one is more open to a charge of hypocrisy than he. Every pastor knows the meaning of moral failure, yet his calling is to summon others to a perfection that he himself has not attained. How can we preach a level of holiness that we have not reached? How can we represent God when, as yet, we fall short of His standard? Indeed, this is not only true of spiritual nonentities. Spurgeon, Whitefield, and other mighty servants of God were painfully aware of this tension between their calling on the one hand, and their lack of holiness on the other. Moses knew it too. How frustrating! A preacher of repentance who needed to repent; a messenger of mercy who needed to be forgiven.

It is not so with Jesus. He is the builder of the house. He is no mere labourer, but the architect. He is on a different level altogether. He is *worthy of more glory than Moses* (3). Verse 4 tells us that the whole project is the work of God. This reminds us that Jesus, though a man, is more than a man. When we preach the gospel and invite men and women to put their trust in Christ, we are not commending them to someone like ourselves. If the best that fallible men could do was to recommend people to follow other fallible men, our situation would be hopeless. We can have confidence in the gospel for this very reason. No prophet or teacher will satisfy the needs of the human soul. The best of them are human themselves! Instead, we call men and women to Jesus. He transcends all human limitations!

Another important difference (4-6)

In the Old Testament it was a rare and precious thing to be
called a servant of God. Moses, we are told in verse 5, was one
of the few who achieved that privileged title. Even so, that is all
he was: a servant in someone else's house. By contrast, as
verse 6 tells us, Christ is *a son over His own house*. How are we
to understand the ministry of Moses? His task was to point the
way; (note verse 5: *for a testimony of those things which would
be spoken afterwards*). Moses resembled someone even greater.
His work had several aspects to it: he was a prophet, a
redeemer, and a ruler over the people. In each of these areas
he prefigured someone who would surpass him in every way.
Moreover, Moses knew it (see Deuteronomy 18:15).

Jesus is the One to whom Moses pointed. No prophet
revealed the truth of God more fully than he did. He has
redeemed the people of God from a bondage worse than the
brick kilns of Egypt. No subjects ever had better prospects than
those who have such a King to rule over them. This is because
Jesus is no mere servant. He is unique. He is the Son of God
from the beginning, 'begotten of the Father before all worlds'.
The church is his because he is the heir. She is his by right.
Sinful human beings have the privilege of entering the house.
Jesus owns it. There is a gold mine of teaching here. These
verses remind us of the mystery of Jesus' person. As builder of
the house he is God. As a Son in the house, he is man. He is
both a human servant of his Father, and at the same time, he is
God, the master of all servants. Oh, consider this Jesus.
Consider him as the unique God-man. The church exists
because he brought her into being. She exists for his pleasure,
and he her head. Look at him in all his perfection, high above
all praises. We venerate great men, and thank God for them,
but Jesus is above them all. Nowadays people despise the church
of Christ. Its numbers are few, and it is divided. The army is a

pathetic rabble. Never mind: look instead at *the Apostle and High Priest of our confession*, look at the Captain, consider Jesus. He has no need of us. Our disarray is not a problem to him. He can, if he so chooses, accomplish his purposes all by himself.

Verse 6 tells us that we are his house. Our cause is a great cause, for he is a great leader. But beware of complacency! The word *if* stares us in the face here. We end with a warning; (it is developed in the rest of the chapter). There is more to following Jesus than making a good beginning. Indeed we must begin! Have we come to Christ at all? How can we tell? Those who do, continue. *They hold fast the confidence and the rejoicing of the hope firm to the end.* Do not be proud because once upon a time you decided to follow Jesus. By itself that is not enough. Has it led on to more? Are you at this moment confident in Christ? Is he your joy and your hope for the future? When you are tempted to wonder if it is really worthwhile, do you train yourself to consider your captain? 'Turn your eyes upon Jesus.'

8
BE FAITHFUL!

Please read Hebrews 3:7-19

Introduction

The Hebrew believers who had first received this epistle had begun well. However, an alarming situation had developed. They were wavering. A crisis had arisen, and a conflict of loyalties had followed. Their Christian profession had brought them into conflict with their fellow Jews. It is a sad fact that all believers fall short of the perfection that God calls them to, and perhaps this stage of uncertainty was no more than that. However, another alarming possibility had occurred to the author. Some people profess faith and then depart from it (12). This is as true now as it was then. As we observe the evangelical scene today, we see people who start out on the Christian life, but after some time has gone by the faith they once professed seems to have evaporated. What are we to make of such people? If they return to disciplined Christian living, the answer is clear. On the other hand there are some who wander and never return. Is it possible for a converted person to cease to be a Christian? Decidedly not. Jesus himself tells us that he would lose none of those whom the Father has given to him, but he will raise them up at the last day (John 8:39). Instead we must face the awful thought that some who claim to be believers are not. They convince others, and perhaps they convince themselves, yet their profession is without foundation.

This leaves us facing an obvious question: how can we detect a true disciple? Verse 6 has the answer. We can be sure that we belong to the household of God *if* we continue. In the same way verse 14 tells us that people with a share in Christ are those who hold on to their confidence *steadfast to the end*. If a person is genuinely converted to Christ there will be a beginning, and there will be a life that follows on from that beginning.

An example to avoid

The author wished to challenge his readers to be faithful to their profession, and so prove that it was real. In verses 1-6 he told them of Moses who was faithful in God's service. Jesus, the *'Apostle and High Priest of their confession'* (1) was faithful too. With those two examples of faithful service before them he goes on from verses 7-11 to give an example of a different sort. In these verses he quotes from Psalm 95: 7-11.

Today, if you will hear His voice, Do not harden your hearts, as in the rebellion, In the day of trial in the wilderness, Where your fathers tested Me, proved Me, And saw My works forty years. Therefore I was angry with that generation, And said, 'They always go astray in their heart, And they have not known my ways.' So I swore in My wrath, 'They shall not enter My rest.'

This psalm is a call to worship. At this point, it challenges the worshippers not to fall into the attitude of their ancestors in the wilderness. The psalm says that it is dangerous to harden our hearts. That is what happened to the generation that left Egypt with Moses. The actual incident to which the psalm refers took place at Rephidim, the last place where the people of Israel stopped on their Exodus from Egypt, before they arrived at Mount Sinai (see Exodus 17:1; 19:2; Numbers 33:14-15). The people were thirsty, and rebellious. Moses, at God's command, struck a rock with his staff and water poured out. Moses called the place Massah (Exodus 17:7). This means *place of testing*. It was not God who was on trial, however. He also named it Meribah (verse 7), which conveys the idea that bitterness of spirit had led to a rebellion against God. (Meribah is taken from a Hebrew word, which means to strive or to complain.) The psalmist mentioned this because it was not an isolated incident. In fact it was typical of the forty years Israel had wandered in the wilderness. They had acted stubbornly again and again.

In passing let us note that a monastic movement among the Jews, the Essenes, was very influential at the time when the epistle to the Hebrews was written. They took the view that the wilderness was a glorious period, a time when the Israelites were free of corruption. They were not exposed to the temptations of material prosperity and the urban life. The Essenes encouraged their followers to form communes in wild and solitary places. Like other monastic movements ever since, they ignored one vital fact. You can leave the city behind, but you take yourself with you. This really stands out from the story of the Exodus. As they moved from place to place the Israelites took their attitudes and problems with them. We need to remember this today when some people are telling us that communion with nature is the answer to all the evils of modern society. Of course fresh air and scenery can be a wonderful tonic. Few things refresh the jaded, overworked mind more than solitude and natural beauty. At the same time, we need to face up to the fact that our greatest problem lies inside us. We can get away from stress with a change of scene. We cannot get away from a sinful heart as easily as that.

Why is the example of the Exodus relevant? The explanation is in 4:2. The Hebrew readers of this epistle and its modern readers too, share something with Moses' companions. The gospel was preached to them and us. At first sight this might seem strange. How could people 2,000 years before the coming of Christ hear the gospel? Nevertheless, we need to grasp that the message of Moses was indeed the gospel. It was not as clear as it is to those who have the benefit of the New Testament, but every element of the gospel was present in Moses' preaching. This is clearly apparent if we look at Exodus 6:6-8.

> Therefore say to the children of Israel: 'I am the LORD; I will bring you out from under the burdens of the Egyptians, I will rescue you from their bondage, and I will redeem you with an outstretched arm and with great judgements. I will take you as My people, and I will be your God. Then you shall know that I am the LORD your God who brings you out from under the burdens of the Egyptians. And I will bring you into the land which I swore to give to Abraham, Isaac, and Jacob; and I will give it to you as a heritage: I am the LORD.'

Here Moses proclaims the message of God to the Israelites in Egypt. It begins with an invitation. The people are in bondage. God offers them release. Indeed the story of the Passover in Exodus 12 adds another dimension to this. God was about to visit a dreadful calamity on the land of Egypt. It was the city of destruction (as in Bunyan's 'The Pilgrim's Progress'), and the people were being invited to flee from the wrath to come. Moses' preaching does not stop there. Once released from their captivity the people are to enter a relationship with God. He is to be their God, and they are to belong to him. He has a claim upon them. They must live for him. Finally Moses taught that they would be brought to a land where they would experience permanent rest and security.

What went wrong in the wilderness?

Escape from destruction, a life of service to God, and never-ending rest – Moses taught these things as a complete whole. He never separated these elements. We must not imagine him saying: 'This is a simple gospel. It is all about freedom. God is giving you a chance to get out of Egypt. That is all there is to it! The other things are optional. Walking with God in the wilderness; that's one of God's advanced courses. You can think about it later.' Moses was faithful in his communication of the gospel. He did not offer people a shrunken version of God's message.

All the people who left Egypt with Moses, except Joshua, Caleb and the children born on their journey to Canaan, perished in the desert. They were not permitted to come to God's rest. In verse 19 we are told that this was because of unbelief. This poses a problem. We assume that they must have had faith in God. They left Egypt at his invitation, and witnessed his miracles! On the other hand verse 18 tells us that the reason they did not enter Canaan was actually disobedi-ence, which was in turn the fruit of their unbelief. At this stage we must move with extreme caution. It would be easy to get the wrong impression altogether. Every earnest Christian knows the meaning of failure. Some even fail in a spectacular manner, as the apostle Peter did. Does verse 18 teach that a person who sins after he has come to Christ immediately loses his pardon and is back where he began? The point to note is that the Greek word translated 'did not obey' is often used in Scripture. However it is never used to describe the sins and failures of true believers. This is a long way from saying that sin does not matter. It always matters! Some believers will not be rewarded as others are as a consequence of their sin, but while they lose their reward, they will not lose salvation itself.

That word 'disobey' is always used of those who reject God. One case in point is Romans 10:21. Paul quotes Isaiah to explain God's rejection of Israel. He rejected them only after bearing patiently with their stubborn rejection of him for a very long period of time. A similar reference comes in 1 Peter 4:17. Unbelievers are described as those *who do not obey the gospel*. We are now in a position to understand why God rejected the Israelites in the wilderness. Our quotation from Psalm 95 has another passage in mind (Numbers 14:11, 22-23). This records God's judgement on the people of Israel. They were not being condemned for a momentary lapse. They had resisted the Lord at every turn. They were chronically disobedient, so much so that it made their claim to faith look shallow. Verses 18 and 19 of Hebrews 3 do not contradict each other. God did not condemn them for two separate things, unbelief and disobedience. The two things go together. Those who believe obey. If people profess faith yet resist God when he requires something of them, it is doubtful whether they have true faith.

When Moses preached the gospel, he did not merely invite the people who left Egypt to lay down their burdens. He also called them to take up the yoke of service. His message from God to Pharaoh was *Let My people go, that they may serve Me* (Exodus 7:16).

Why it matters

The author of Hebrews quoted Psalm 95 so that we might consider the real state of those who died in Sinai. They had been through a religious crisis. On the strength of it they had enjoyed some remarkable blessings. Even so, it did not last. As they did not continue, we must ask ourselves whether they really began in the first place. This question challenged the first century believers who received this letter. They, like us, had a better revelation than the one God gave through Moses. They had made a response to it. Was that response genuine? This challenge has lost none of its force, for there are still people who seem to be believers but who are not.

In part the phenomenon of 'temporary believers' results from a certain kind of preaching. For some decades, a version of the gospel has been preached which is defective because it does not present the total picture. Perhaps it was popular because of a desire to proclaim the truth in a way that was clear and uncomplicated. By all means let us be simple, but the 'simple gospel' actually presents only part of the message. People are told that the gospel is about forgiveness and no more. They are encouraged to come to Jesus and be saved. This is all very necessary. Indeed people must come to Christ! Let us urge them to do so. If anyone reading these words has not been reconciled to God, I plead with you: get right with him! Call upon him, plead with him for mercy. At the same time there is more. This is apparent in Jesus' tender invitation in Matthew 11:28–30.

> Come to Me, all you who labour and are heavy laden, and I will give you rest. Take My yoke upon you and learn from Me, for I am gentle and lowly in heart, and you will find rest for your souls. For My yoke is easy and My burden is light.

Here is a tender invitation from Jesus himself. Are you burdened with a sense of sin and guilt? Jesus bids you come to him. He also calls upon you to take up his yoke. Holy living is not an option for advanced candidates or spiritual enthusiasts. If a preacher ever tells you that the lordship of Christ over your entire life is something that is an extra, and not an essential part of the gospel, that preacher is a heretic. He is encouraging faith without obedience.

We must also reckon with our own hearts at this point. As verse 13 says, sin is deceitful. Some tragic individuals are deceived into thinking that they are converted because of an incident long ago. They recall a traumatic moment. Emotion was running high; the atmosphere was intense. They made a commitment. However all this is years in the past, and the present reality is so different. They profess faith, but their life is not consistent with their profession. In the meantime, they cling to their memory of that occasion and reassure themselves that that is enough. They may well have been baptised or become a church member on the strength of that dramatic incident. Even so, being converted without a change of heart is not conversion to Christ.

One aspect of this is especially frightening: verse 13 calls it hardening. The Greek word is related to our word 'sclerosis'. How graphic! Someone eats too much fatty food, and as time passes the arteries clog and the blood vessels become like furred up water pipes. The supply of blood becomes sluggish; life is threatened. In the same way spiritual hardening is insidious, slow and fatal. All the while a person claims to be a child of God. At the same time he resists the promptings of God's Spirit, and little by little, his sensitivity to spiritual things becomes less. Eventually it becomes clear that the outward life shows the true state of a heart that was never right with God at all. How awful! Let the Hebrews beware! Let us also beware!

9
ENTERING GOD'S REST

Please read Hebrews 4:1-13

Introduction

One of the most attractive words in the Bible is *rest*. It has a particular appeal to people living in a world of turmoil and bustle. The idea of freedom from stress is enticing. However, when the Bible speaks of rest, it means more than the absence of activity. It is not the kind of rest that comes when we stop doing something, but a condition of being completely at peace with the world and with oneself. It grows from being at peace with God. Hebrews chapter 4 tells us that this rest is something that God promises. It is not a figment of the imagination. It can be known and enjoyed. At the same time it is not something that everyone enjoys as of right as the author of the epistle makes clear. He feared lest his readers should *come short of it* (1). In the same way he encouraged them to be *diligent to enter that rest* (11). There is a real danger of complacency. We can be as prone to it as Jewish Christians in the first century were! Take notice! Ahead of us is the possibility of entering God's wonderful rest. But can we be confident of it?

The promise of rest is part of the gospel

The theme of this chapter carries on from that of chapter three. In that chapter the author quoted from Psalm 95, which referred to the people of Israel in the wilderness. He did so because they left an example that we do well to avoid. They failed to enter God's rest. This was because of their faithless response to the gospel. As verse 2 says, they heard the gospel just as the author and his readers did, and just as we do today. Sadly, they neither believed it (2), nor obeyed it (11), which amounts to the same thing! Admittedly they did not hear it with the clarity of the New Testament revelation, but it was still the gospel that they heard. There is a summary of this gospel in Exodus 6:6-8, as we have seen in the previous chapter. Moses preached to the people in Egypt and gave them a message with several elements. It begins with a message of hope to people in captivity. God can release them! God offered more than freedom to the Israelites, and called them to more than service. He also promised them rest. The same elements are always present in true gospel preaching.

Moses' gospel was only a shadowy picture of something yet to come. It pointed forward. The author reasons that God's rest must consist of something more than physical safety and prosperity in Palestine. First of all, verse 6 says that the people who heard Moses' message did not enter God's rest. In addition, verse 8 says that those who entered Canaan under the leadership of Joshua did not achieve all that there was to achieve. If God had only meant that they would be freed from their enemies, why did he say that his rest was still there to be won? We see in verse 7 that as in chapter three the author refers to Psalm 95. When the psalm was written this rest was something that could be gained *today*. For the Hebrew believers it was still *today,* and so it is for us. Verse 9 sums it up: *there remains a rest for the people of God.*

At this stage we must grasp the fact that the Old Testament and New Testament do not teach different messages. The Bible is one book, inspired by a gracious God who proclaims the same truth throughout. Nevertheless the New Testament provides a picture that is much clearer than that of the Old Testament. The New Testament shows that the people of God have escaped a worse bondage than slavery in Egypt. Resourceful individuals might have slipped away from Pharaoh's brick-kilns, but the captivity of sin has bound us with chains that we cannot break. Furthermore, the wrath of God that fell upon Egypt on Passover night is as nothing compared to the destruction that he will bring upon a sinful world when the accounts are finally settled. We must heed the old message: 'Flee from the wrath to come'! Also the gospel, as it is taught in the New Testament, lays the same emphasis on the need to begin a new life of service to God. It adds the extra dimension that it is Jesus whom we must follow through the wilderness of this world. Finally the prospect of rest is very much part of the picture, but nothing as fleeting as mere outward peace and safety. Canaan, the land of corn and wine, milk and honey, beautiful as it undoubtedly was, is only a dim outline of the happy country that awaits believers. *Eye has not seen, nor ear heard, nor have entered into the heart of man the things which God has prepared for those who love Him* (1 Corinthians 2:9).

What makes this state of rest so attractive? To be fully at rest is to be where God is. Verse 4 quotes Genesis 2:2. When the six days of creation were over, God rested. This does not mean that he ceased to do anything. As Jesus said, *My Father has been working until now, and I have been working* (John 5:17). It means instead that God began to enjoy what he had made. The seventh day, the day of God's rest, is still with us. (The Genesis account says that the other six days came to an end, but not the Sabbath). To enter rest is to enter that state where God takes pleasure in all that is his. Perfect rest means living in intimate communion with God, enjoying him, and knowing his approval. Who knows, those who rest may turn out to be busy! God is busy even now sustaining the world and carrying out his purposes. After all, rest is not idleness but contentment. A man in an armchair may be in a state of hopeless turmoil, while someone who is extremely busy may be at peace. Rest still beckons! That urgent word *Today* tells us that the opportunity to enjoy it is not over. To people uncomfortable because of sin, Jesus says: *Come to me, and I will give you rest* (Matthew 11:28).

What is involved in winning God's rest?

It is not enough to want it! Lots of people like the idea of heaven but never go there. Imagine the response Moses would have got if he'd gone round saying no more than: 'How would you like to live in a land of milk and honey?' Who would refuse such an invitation! Nor should it surprise us that people respond in great numbers to some preachers. Their message begins and ends with an invitation to receive pardon and go to heaven. This is a cheap travesty of the gospel. Along with the offer of pardon, we must reckon with something else.

Let us consider the example of the Israelites in the wilderness once more. As soon as they crossed the Jordan they would begin to enjoy the fruit of the land. Even so, it would be a long while before they enjoyed rest on every side, because there was work to be done. There were enemies to subdue. This was the point at which it all went wrong for the Israelites. As soon as the spies they sent into Canaan brought back news of the enemy forces, their resolution faded. The price was too high. The prospect of a series of battles against the gigantic sons of Anak was enough to make them long for Egypt once again. This incident provoked God into disqualifying those people from entering the rest of Canaan (Numbers 13:17-33).

Jesus warned against making the same mistake. His parable of the man who built a tower without checking his stock of materials is one example (Luke 14:28-30), as is the story of the king who provoked his neighbour into war without ensuring that his army was strong enough to be sure of victory (Luke 14:31-32). Unlike the dying thief, we do not enter heaven immediately we are converted. In consequence we must adjust to the idea that we are to live for Jesus, and this can be arduous. Spiritual obstacles lie in the path as daunting as the Anakims and their iron chariots were to the Israelites (Numbers 13:33). There is more to Christianity than a statement of preferences. Of course you would sooner go to heaven than to hell. Who wouldn't? But are you prepared for what that will mean? Will you follow Jesus wherever he leads? This is the reason for the stress on diligence in verse 11. Those who have quit the fight have a question mark hanging over them. They might be the sort of people who come short of God's rest! At this point we would do well to consider Paul's words in Philippians 3:13-14.

> Brethren, I do not count myself to have apprehended; but one thing I do, forgetting those things which are behind and reaching forward to those things which are ahead, I press toward the goal for the prize of the upward call of God in Christ Jesus.

We often use this text to comfort ourselves when we have failed. Forgiveness means that a fresh start is always available. Nevertheless, forgetting what is behind is also a powerful challenge to spiritual reality. What is the good of a decision made years ago if we are not living as disciples now? Yesterday's good resolutions are worth no more than last week's successes. If we profess faith in Christ we must prove it. Let us press on!

Sorting the wheat from the chaff

Undoubtedly some people are on their way to God's rest. Equally, some deceive themselves. It is not always difficult to detect such people. The Israelites claimed to belong to God, but resisted his will for forty years. At other times however, discerning whether people have deceived themselves is not so straightforward. This was true of the Hebrews who first received this letter. As the author wrote he was conscious of uneasiness about them, and hoped they would not become complacent. We may find it difficult to read the hearts of some people who profess to be Christians, but God knows exactly where everyone stands.

Verse 12 tells us that the word of God is *living and powerful*. The Bible is more than ink on paper. It has the ability to lay bare the interior of the human personality. The illustration of the two-edged sword is very telling. Few things were sharper in those days than the double-edged 'gladius' of the Roman legionary. It was an awesome weapon in the hand of a trained soldier, penetrating right to the vital organs of an adversary. God's word can cut deeper still! Incidentally, some have taken the reference to the *division of soul and spirit* to mean that soul and spirit are distinct components of our make-up as human beings. The author's intention, however, was not so much to make a point about human nature as to describe the power of the word of God in overcoming our resistance. The idea is simply this: God's word can pierce to the hidden depths of the human soul. It discerns the *thoughts and intents of the heart*. As verse 13 shows, the outer defences are stripped bare. God reveals to us things that we hide from others and even from ourselves. This is why it is imperative that we bring people to hear preaching. Leave them undisturbed and they will go comfortably and cosily to hell. *Those who are well have no need of a physician but those who are sick* (Matthew 9:12), and they will never cry to God for mercy until they become aware of the diseased state of their souls. The word of God will peel off layer after layer until the truth is apparent.

Is it any wonder that some people react against preaching? The word of God opens wounds that smart. Many of us have vivid memories of squirming in agony as the piercing blade probed our innermost recesses. We know how it feels to tell God to stop interfering, to keep off, to leave us alone and go away. Why does modern Christianity have a tendency to de-value preaching? No doubt it stems in part from the fact that much preaching nowadays is bad, and some who know no better conclude that there must be a better alternative. How-ever, some of it is the result of fear, the desire to silence that insistent voice that fills the inward ear with dread.

This is where the difference between the believer and the unbeliever shows up. Look at John 3:19-21.

> And this is the condemnation, that the light has come into the world, and men loved darkness rather than light, because their deeds were evil. For everyone practicing evil hates the light and does not come to the light, lest his deeds should be exposed. But he who does the truth comes to the light, that his deeds may be clearly seen, that they have been done in God.

A real Christian loves the Bible, the Word of God. This does not mean that he always likes it. He too will sometimes writhe under it, but he has come to learn that this is necessary. He has learned to see sin as God sees it, and wants to be rid of it. He steels himself to face up to the probing searchlight of Scripture. The unbeliever is like the insects that scuttle away when you turn on the light. Have you been running away from God? You cannot hide for ever. Come to the light, submit to the surgery. It is the only way. The Christian life begins when we come to Jesus and truly confess our sin. It continues in the same way.

Again and again we come to the Saviour. Over and over we confront our sin and seek to root it out. At conversion God forgives sin and that for ever. Equally it marks the beginning of an unremitting war against personal sin in all its forms. Those who habitually and continually shirk this contest will never enter the rest that God has prepared for his people.

10
JESUS – THE GREAT HIGH PRIEST

Please read Hebrews 4:14-16

Introduction

These three verses introduce a new and lengthy section of the epistle. It will occupy our attention until well into the tenth chapter. So far, we have found that the epistle makes a series of comparisons: Jesus is greater than the prophets, the angels, and even Moses. Now we find yet another point of comparison. Jesus is greater than Aaron and the priests of his line. This matters enormously, because we need a priest. We cannot approach God without one. As we have observed in chapters 3 and 4 God has standards. He expects a great deal of those who would serve him. He requires consistency. If we know ourselves at all, we will know that we often fail miserably. Certainly the first readers of this letter were conscious of their failings. Their circumstances were forbidding. They got no sympathy from friends and relations. However, it was not this hostility which proved their biggest problem. God himself seemed so unrelenting. His holiness was unattainable. Which ordinary mortal could live with the unceasing call for perfection? According to this passage there is no need to come before the Almighty as though he were one of Pharaoh's taskmasters. We can draw near to God, and do so with composure and confidence. Our sin need not debar us. There is someone who can satisfy an offended

God, and who provides an offering that God will accept. As needy as we are, we have a priest, a great high priest. His name is Jesus.

An exalted High Priest (14)

First century Judaism deserves our respect, for it took sin seriously. The centrepiece of the whole system was the temple with its endless succession of sacrifices. No mere man could draw near to God without an oblation, an offering to offset his guilt. No doubt at this point, those who remained faithful to Judaism often chided the early Christians. 'You have no priest! How can you get right with God, if no one can mediate for you?' Perhaps we have heard the same accusation? Our religion has a fatal flaw, we are told. Nobody is acceptable to God unless he enlists the aid of specially qualified individuals to perform the mysterious rituals that clear the path.

Believers then had their Jewish critics, and we have ours from within Christendom. They despise our simplicity, and tell us to cultivate the same grandeur that they affect. Their criticisms need not trouble us, for we do have a priest. He is a *great high priest* (14). This phrase is interesting. The Hebrew expression translated 'high priest' means 'great priest'. Thus, it follows that Jesus is a 'great, great priest'. His priesthood is superlative. He is an illustrious priest, a splendid priest, a priest like no other.

We are also told that he has *passed through the heavens*. This reminds us of the high priests of Israel. Every year, on the 'Day of Atonement', they went into the holy place in the temple and then passed through the veil into the most holy place. They left the world of men behind and passed into the nearer presence of God. At this point the similarity ends. The high priests of long ago always returned. Their time in the presence of God was purely temporary. The problem lay with the offerings that they made. They were not adequate. The blood of bulls and goats could never take away sins (10:4). What then, was the point of these sacrifices, given that the death of an animal is not an adequate substitute for the death of a human being? The sacrifices of the Old Testament era pointed forward to the much greater offering that took place at Calvary, when the Lord Jesus Christ made an offering that God would accept in the sacrifice of himself. The sin of believers before the coming of Christ was atoned for not by the blood of bulls and goats, but by the blood of Christ, which was symbolised by the blood of beasts slaughtered on the altar of the temple in Jerusalem. Because Jesus' sacrifice was acceptable to God, there was no need for him to repeat it. It need not trouble us that we cannot see our priest. Nor need we feel troubled by those who insist on a regular sacrifice in the form of the Mass. Jesus' sacrifice of himself was enough to satisfy the demands of God's justice. God has accepted both high priest and offering.

This verse reminds us that Jesus is the Son of God. This makes all the difference. The priests of ancient Israel were inadequate partly because of their very humanity. In common with the rest of mankind they were sinners. This was a handicap. Before they could atone for the sins of others, they had to atone for their own sins. Every human being who has ever lived needs a priest. We are guilty before God. We need someone to take our part. Unfortunately, there is no priest on the face of the earth entirely free from guilt. How are we helped if those who would represent us are as guilty as we are? This is why people with spiritual understanding turn away from other priests to Jesus. He is the only priest who can bring an offering to God that is satisfactory in every way. Look at his life! There is not one instance of sinful behaviour against his record, for this priest is the holy God in human form. My life is a miserable record of failure, and all the priests of Israel and Christendom have that in common with me. God is willing to accept Jesus' life as though it were my own. Look at his death! This is not the death of a brute beast, however spotless. It is the voluntary death of a human being. How can the death of an animal take the place of mine? But this high priest offers an offended God a human life in exchange for others. Truly he is a great high priest! Whoever comes to this priest will never want to resort to any other. Why should we *hold fast to our confession* (14)? We have a Saviour worth confessing.

In passing, let us observe that the person who has passed through the heavens is Jesus. We deny the idea, popular today, that Jesus was only a man upon whom the 'Christ spirit' came at the time of his baptism. The man on the throne of heaven was the baby of Bethlehem.

A sympathetic High Priest (15)

Some people think that a person with a privileged background cannot really help ordinary people. We often say of such people: 'They don't know how the other half lives'. Are you ever tempted to think that way about Jesus? 'How could a divine being understand me? We live in different worlds! My struggles and problems can mean nothing to him'.

This is where we do well to consider the humanity of our priest. In saying that he was more than human, we are not saying that he was less than human. His human nature was not a mask. He did not pretend to be a man, he was a man. He experienced all that we experience except for sin. This is more than saying that he shared the physical aspects of human life, hunger, thirst, pain and so on. He experienced temptations, for he underwent the same temptation as those Hebrew believers. He was tempted to commit apostasy, to fall away from the service of God. He heard that temptation from the lips of Peter, who told him that he should reject the very idea of suffering and crucifixion. The most poignant example is the agony in the garden (Luke 22:39-46). There he fought the desire to turn away from suffering and death. On the cross his enemies taunted him and told him to come down and save himself (Matthew 27:42-43; Luke 23:35-37). In a hundred different ways we are faced with the enticing idea of leaving God's service. Depend upon it, this temptation will never go away altogether. Satan never strays far from believers. Next time you are tempted to give way to the seductive promptings of the evil one, remind yourself that your high priest can feel for you because he too has been confronted by the same temptation.

In our worst moments we can be tempted to say,' It wasn't the same for him. He didn't sin!' While it is true that the Son of God was sinless, this does not mean that he could not feel the intensity of temptation itself. It is not as though Jesus is sinless because he was never tested. That would be a cheap victory. Temptation faces us and we fail. It faced him and he won. He achieved his record of perfect holiness against a background of grievous testing and constant trials. Where we fail, he succeeded. Indeed, he felt the power of it more acutely than we do. Failure has deadened us. There was a time when we were more sensitive to sin, but giving in to it numbs our spiritual senses. Our capacity to resist is blunted. This is a matter of everyday experience. People become hardened to things that once made them think more than twice. This explains the paradox of Christian growth: as the believer advances in holiness, he actually feels worse. This is because he has begun to recover his sensitivity to sin. It may seem strange, but the person who senses his wretchedness is on the way to recovery. He has learned to see sin as God sees it, and that is progress.

Let us not misunderstand: our High Priest knows how we feel. Our frailties are not beyond him. He does not look down on us in scorn. It is dispiriting if someone says 'Stop acting like this!' Inside ourselves we respond 'It's all right for you, you don't know what it's like!' The fact that our Saviour is human is a reminder that he does know. Satan whispered in his ear too, and because he was sinless he felt the sharpness of it all the more. There is nothing detached or aloof about our high priest. *He knows our frame; He remembers that we are dust* (Psalm 103:14). Some people seek the services of a priest when they need sympathy, but who could be more sympathetic than this priest? He knows our situation from his own experience, and with perfect understanding.

> Our fellow-sufferer yet retains,
> A fellow-feeling of our pains,
> And still remembers in the skies
> His tears, His agonies, and cries.

> (Michael Bruce, 1746-67)

A High Priest who gives confidence (16)

Verse 16 invites us to picture ourselves coming before God's throne with boldness. It reminds us of the story of Esther. The time came when she had to approach King Artaxerxes, the sole ruler of an empire whose dominions stretched from Greece to India. He had the power of life and death, and Esther was not certain of the reception she would get. In the ancient world a throne had a single purpose. It was intended to exalt the one who sat on it, to make him seem remote, even terrifying. Ordinary people were made to feel their own smallness and insignificance compared with the exalted being on the throne. Esther would have been very apprehensive. As it turned out, the king held out the golden sceptre, a gesture of favour, and all went well. She did not approach the throne of Persia with boldness, but with fear. Fortunately, if only for a moment, it was a throne of grace.

If we talk of coming to God in this manner, some people will accuse us of presumption. However we do not argue that there is something special about us, and that we believe that God will recognise our merits. Who could be confident, if all they had to show God was their list of poor achievements? Even the best of us is a failure, who has come short of the glory of God. The Christian does not base his confidence on his own worth. Indeed if you want to approach God in this assured way, only Jesus can give you grounds for doing so. The believer knows that Jesus has lived the life that he could not live, and died to pay the penalty for his sin. Such a person no longer enters the presence of God as an offender. That awesome throne is no longer just a symbol of power and authority, but one of welcome too.

If Jesus is your High Priest you can draw near to God and be sure of mercy. He has completely forgiven the past, with all its regrets, the wrongdoing and omissions, the guilt and moral failure. Furthermore, we can approach God confident of his help in the future. There is *grace to help in time of need*. This does not mean that God does everything through us as though we were spiritual robots. This verse takes a realistic view of the various circumstances of life.

From time to time God places us in situations where we need help, and makes us feel it. Sometimes he places us in such situations in order to teach us this very lesson. God is more concerned about the quality of our relationship with him than with the things we do or don't get done. Now and again we need to learn again how much we depend on him. The world is full of pitfalls. The spiritual realist knows that he will need help. But where are we to find help? Because of Jesus, help is available from the best source of all: the throne of omnipotence is the throne of grace, where limitless kindness and limitless power can both be found. Remember also that the One who occupies that throne is not merely favourable toward us, he is one of us, and knows just how it feels. Is this Jesus your priest? You can only say yes to that question if you have learned to 'confess' him, to acknowledge that you are lost and helpless without him, that you depend upon him entirely and alone for salvation, and that you seek to follow him as his willing servant. Will you not approach God through his appointed high priest? No other mediator will do. Jesus, and he alone, is the great High Priest.

11
JESUS – THE RIGHT HIGH PRIEST

Please read Hebrews 5:1-11

Introduction

The central chapters of this epistle are unique in Scripture, teaching something that is found nowhere else. They portray Jesus as the High Priest of his people. This theme begins in the closing verses of chapter 4, where we are told that Jesus is a high priest who is both great and compassionate. Now, in the opening verses of chapter 5, he is shown to be the right High Priest, the one ideally fitted for his task. We can have complete confidence in him, for in every respect he is altogether suitable.

The qualifications for High Priesthood

Why do we need a high priest at all? Verse 1 explains this for us. A high priest is *appointed for men in things pertaining to God*. If human beings are to approach God they need a representative, someone to act on their behalf. This mediation is necessary because of sin. God's creatures have offended him, and until the offence is removed, there can be no fellowship. Verse 2 shows us two sides to sin. Sometimes we sin because of ignorance. We do not know what we are doing. This is not an excuse: it is our duty to know what God requires of us. We also sin knowingly; we know the path and go astray from it. (In passing, let us note that the Old Testament sacrifices allowed for those who were aware of their sin, and those who sinned unwittingly. There was no sacrifice for those who sinned *with a high hand* [see Numbers 15:27ff]. As we shall see from chapter 6, that principle still stands. Those who defy God blatantly and continually put themselves beyond the reach of mercy).

This picture of humanity is depressingly accurate. We blunder around in wilful ignorance. Even when we do know what God expects, we go astray. God is indignant, and will not accept us unless something is done to placate him. It would be easy to get the wrong impression here. A man comes home late from work. The dinner will be ruined, and his wife upset, so he buys her some flowers as a peace-offering. It is not so with God! The *gifts and sacrifices* mentioned here are not presents aimed at keeping God sweet, but his appointed way of recognising guilt and dealing with it. Sin incurs a penalty. A just God cannot overlook this principle. That is why Old Testament sacrifices did not merely consist of offerings of food, but, at God's direction, included animals too. *For the life of the flesh is in the blood, and I have given it to you upon the altar to make atonement for your souls; for it is the blood that makes atonement for the soul.* (Leviticus 17:11) If God were to be reconciled to those who deserved his wrath, a price had to be paid, a life in place of their own. This is our position too. We have no hope of appearing before God unless we have a high priest to provide an offering that God will accept. We need a high priest more than anything else! The message of this epistle is that God, in his mercy, has provided both the high priest and the offering that we needed.

It is extremely important that the person in question should be a man himself. He should be *taken from among men.* Only someone who is one of us can represent us! (This is why the animal sacrifices of the Old Testament era were symbols, which pointed forward to the sacrifice of Christ. That sacrifice was effective in a way that they could never be. A bull or goat is no substitute for a man or woman). The priests of Israel were sinners themselves. Although their office was important they had no grounds for pride. They were prone to the same weaknesses as their neighbours.

Further, it was not enough to have the right personal qualities. Some people nowadays become ministers in the same way that others become lawyers or doctors. They see it as an attractive profession that will bring much personal fulfilment. According to verse 4, no one in Old Testament days became a priest in that spirit. The priest had to receive a call from God. Only Aaron and his descendants in the tribe of Levi had received this call. This was a big issue in the first century. King Herod the Great had appointed his own friends to the priesthood. Old Testament history shows God's attitude to such presumption. When Israel wandered in the wilderness three men tried to force themselves into office. One, Korah was not from Aaron's family, and the other two, Dathan and Abiram, were not even from the tribe of Levi. God's disapproval was such that he made the ground open up and swallow them (see Numbers 16:20-35). If a man was to represent the people of God, two qualifications were vital. He had to be a fit and a called high priest.

Jesus, fit to be our High Priest

Was Jesus *taken from among men*? He most certainly was. He was born of a human mother, had a body of flesh and blood, and grew up in a human family. Jesus was the *Man of sorrows* (Isaiah 53:3). He died as a man at Calvary and was buried in the tomb at Golgotha. Verse 7 speaks of *the days of his flesh*. Our mediator is no phantom or disembodied spirit, but *the Man Christ Jesus* (1 Timothy 2:5). At this point a question arises:

since he was not only a man, but also a sinless man, how can he truly be one of us? The high priests of Israel could have compassion on fallible men and women because they stood where we stand. How can Jesus know how we feel? He never knew the meaning of failure.

Such questions must not disturb us. If Jesus shared our sin, as well as our humanity, we would be in deep trouble. We do not need the help of a fellow loser. It is vital that our mediator won through at the point where we failed. Verse 9 speaks of his *having been perfected*. This does not mean that he eventually reached perfection after a period of hard struggle, as though there had once been a time when he had not been perfect! At this point, the author is concerned to develop his statement in verse 8 that Jesus *learned obedience by the things which he suffered*. It is a restatement of the truth outlined in 2:10, where we read that the author of our salvation was *made perfect through sufferings*. Throughout his life on earth, the Son of God faced a series of trials. The sharp trial of the cross itself was only the last of many occasions when obedience to his father brought suffering along with it. In the face of each and every trial, Jesus both retained and established his integrity. He obeyed God to the utmost limit, even when God required him, as an innocent man, to bear the punishment for the sin of others. In doing so, he established the integrity of his holy character beyond all doubt. This is why he is called in verse 9 *the author of eternal salvation to all who obey him*. Jesus' perfect life has earned our place in glory, and we can but rejoice in it.

In any case, it would be wrong to think that a record of sinless obedience meant that he knew nothing of suffering. As we have seen, verse 8 says that *He learned obedience by the things which he suffered*. This does not mean that he was like us! We are disobedient by nature, and have to learn. It simply means that he went through the lesson that all godly people have had to learn down the centuries. If we wish to obey God, it will cost us. Obedience brings suffering. We know that all too well, and we shrink from it. The price is too great! At this point let us recognise that we are not on our own. Verse 7 takes us back to Gethsemane. The *vehement cries and tears* of the Son of God were not an act. The emotional intensity of the moment was real. When he asked that the cup might pass from him, he meant every word. As he looks upon his people in the fiery trials of their daily lives, he is no detached observer. He knows, from experience, that godly living can exact a terrible price. God heard his prayer in the end, but he had to pass through death before God rescued him from it. The believer is not exempt from trials. Prayer is not a way of escape from difficulties. The experience of our Saviour, however, guarantees that godly fear has its reward. Beyond the furnace of affliction is God himself, at whose right hand there are pleasures for evermore, and in whose presence there is fullness of joy.

Why is Jesus fit to be his people's high priest? He shares their nature. He represents them as the great victor. As a real man he has won their fight against Satan and sin. At the same time he knows that godly living brings suffering. Our Saviour had to do more than surrender his physical life. He had to endure the condemnation of a holy God. No one before or since, has carried, or could carry, such a load. When we feel the burden of discipleship, can we argue that our high priest knows nothing about it, that it was all right for him? Who better to be our representative, than the desolate man of Gethsemane?

Jesus, called to be our High Priest

A first-century Jew, and perhaps Jews today, would discount all those statements. In spite of his holy life and personal qualities, he had no right to the priesthood. Only members of a single family, out of one particular tribe, could become priests.

Jesus belonged to the tribe of Judah. Admittedly this was the royal line, and Jesus had the bloodline of King David. Nevertheless, he was not a descendant of Aaron. Kings had no more right to serve at the altar than priests had the right to assume royal purple. The story of King Uzziah is instructive (see 2 Chronicles 26:16-23). He went into the temple to offer a sacrifice, and God cursed him with leprosy. He remained a leper until he died. This rigid separation between the monarchy and the priesthood coloured the thinking of the Essenes. That first century Jewish movement, which regarded the wilderness experience as Israel's greatest time of blessing, and encouraged a retreat into monasticism, expected two Messiahs, one a King and the other a priest. It was all quite straightforward: only members of the tribe of Levi were called to the priesthood. As Jesus belonged to the tribe of Judah, he could not have been called by God, and if he claimed to be, he was an intruder.

The writer to the Hebrews answers this from the Old Testament. First of all, in verse 5, he quotes from Psalm 2:7. This psalm concerns the way that God vindicates his anointed servant in the face of opposition. Although the heathen rage, God pronounces that Messiah is his Son. Those who will not make their peace with the Son are in rebellion against the Lord himself! The whole psalm teaches that Messiah is God's anointed king. The next quotation, in verse 6, adds to the picture. It is from Psalm 110:4. This is another messianic psalm. The opening four verses read as follows:

The LORD said to my Lord, 'Sit at My right hand, till I make Your enemies Your footstool.' The LORD shall send the rod of Your strength out of Zion. Rule in the midst of Your enemies! Your people shall be volunteers In the day of Your power; In the beauties of holiness, from the womb of the morning, You have the dew of Your youth. The LORD has sworn and will not relent, 'You are a priest forever According to the order of Melchizedek.'

These verses describe the scene in heaven as the Sovereign Lord welcomes his anointed upon his return from his mission. When we saw a quotation from the same Psalm in Chapter 1 (9), we noted that the author saw this as a reference to God's receiving of the risen Christ in glory. God the Lord bade him occupy the place of honour until his enemies were all vanquished. Once again, this psalm portrays Messiah as the incomparable King. However, in verse 4 the Lord says more. His anointed servant is not only a King, but also a priest, an eternal priest after the order of Melchizedek.

Later the author will say much more on this theme. For the moment let us observe that he deals decisively with the Jewish objection that as Jesus was not from the tribe of Levi, he could not be a priest. He does not claim that Jesus belongs to Aaron's priesthood, but to a greater, more illustrious order. We meet Melchizedek in Genesis 14:18–24. He was *King of Salem* and *priest of God Most High*. He held both offices! Even the patriarch Abraham deferred to him, bringing him an offering from the spoils of his campaign against the four kings. Abraham was an ancestor of Aaron! Our Saviour's priesthood does not stem from the institution of the Passover. Like Melchizedek of old, he unites the functions of King and Priest. As King he rules over and protects his people. As priest he offers the one sacrifice that can atone for their sin. He is a perpetual high priest. As such he cancels the order of Aaronic priests. Their work is over. He has superseded them. A new and better priesthood is in force. We sinners need a priest, a mediator to heal the breach with Almighty God. Only one priest will suffice. We can forget the priests of Israel – their time has passed. We can discount the priests of Christendom. God has only one chosen priest who will never be replaced or superseded. The priest we need is Jesus. He is worthy of the office; God called him to it. Let us make sure that we approach God through his one appointed mediator.

12
SPIRITUAL SECOND CHILDHOOD

Please read Hebrews 5:11-14.

Introduction

The middle chapters of this epistle are concerned with the glory of Christ, and in particular with his ministry as the high priest of his people. The latter part of Chapter 5 and the earlier part of Chapter 6 form a digression from this main theme. The author felt frustrated. He knew that his readers needed this teaching. What could be more encouraging to a believer in trouble than to know that he has a high priest? Think of the apostle Peter. At times he was in such difficulties, that Satan seemed to be sifting him like wheat. What a comfort it must have been to remember the words of the Lord Jesus: *I have prayed for you, that your faith should not fail* (Luke 22:31,32). The believer is never alone! Moreover, this was no ordinary high priest. Jesus was better than all of Aaron's descendants. He was a high priest *according to the order of Melchizedek* (10). The author, however, was troubled. Instead of benefiting from such teaching, his readers were unreceptive.

What had caused this disturbing situation? The problem was not the author's ability to communicate, but his readers' inability to take instruction. They were *dull of hearing* (11). By this the author did not mean that they were deaf, or that their mental capacity was limited. The problem was that they were unwilling to listen. This had not always been the case. They had *become* listless and dull. These Hebrew Christians are an example of something alarming. They prove that Christians can decline. We use the word 'backslider' for such a person. Backsliding is a frightening possibility. We would do well to look at these people because modern Christians are just as likely to backslide as those in the first century.

What 'backsliding' means

Things ought to have been very different. People who had been disciples as long as they had ought to have reached a certain level of maturity. They ought to have been *teachers* (12). This does not mean that every one of them ought to have achieved some responsibility for public ministry. It means that people who had been Christians as long as they had, ought to have been able to share their faith in an intelligible fashion. There was no excuse for such people then, and there is none today. There are believers who excuse their silence before the world by saying: 'I wouldn't know what to say'. Newly converted people may have some justification for saying this but as time goes on they should make progress. Backsliding means that new life is not growing, but withering. It is an abnormal condition. It is neither good nor healthy!

Verse 13 means that the Hebrews were in a state of spiritual babyhood. Does that remind you of moments in your childhood? Did anyone ever say, 'Don't be such a baby!' to you? Perhaps you were being petulant, or were in tears over a trifling injury. How it stung to be told that you were behaving no better than an infant. This is similar to Paul's rebuke to the Corinthian church:

And I, brethren, could not speak to you as to spiritual people but as to carnal, as to babes in Christ. I fed you with milk and not with solid food; for until now you were not able to receive it, and even now you are still not able; for you are still carnal. For where there are envy, strife, and divisions among you, are you not carnal and behaving like mere men? (1 Corinthians 3:1-3)

The behaviour of an infant can be appealing, but it is very annoying to see an adult with the mannerisms of a toddler. The author makes a clear contrast between his readers and *those who are of full age* (14). His challenge was the spiritual equivalent of those common expressions 'Act your age!' and 'Grow up!'

Sometimes old people seem to re-enter childhood. They lapse into patterns of behaviour similar to those of small children. They are no longer what they once were. They have left maturity and responsibility behind. The first recipients of this letter appear to have entered a kind of spiritual second childhood. As such, they are a warning to believers in every age. It would not only be wrong to imagine that such a thing could never happen to us, it would be complacent folly: *Let him who thinks he stands take heed lest he fall* (1 Corinthians 10:12). I gained my Bachelor of Arts degree at Cambridge University in 1973. I was delighted to discover that I could proceed to the Master of Arts degree simply by waiting for 10 more terms to pass by. In due course, I graduated as Master of Arts early in 1977. In effect, any Cambridge student who graduates as Bachelor of Arts will receive a Master's degree. If he waits around long enough, he is sure to get one. Christian progress is not like that. Growth in grace is not guaranteed. In some cases believers go backwards.

What backsliding involves

Backsliding comes about gradually. It does not announce itself with a fanfare of trumpets, and make its presence felt in an instant. It creeps up on us and often catches us by surprise. Nevertheless it leaves certain marks. The first readers of this epistle were showing unmistakable signs, and we must watch for the same symptoms in ourselves.

The first symptom is poor memory. Small children and elderly people often have this in common. Five year old Jonathan wants his jig-saw puzzle. Not unreasonably, his mother asks: 'Where did you put it?' In the same way, while Grandma can remember things that happened when she was a girl, she has no memory of where she put her purse when she came home from the shops. The Hebrew believers of the first century were in much the same position. There were things that they had forgotten so completely that they needed to have them explained all over again. Nor had they forgotten anything particularly complicated or exotic. They were in danger of losing their grip on the *first principles* (12).

If we look ahead to 6:1 we can see what this means. It is as if the author wonders whether it will be necessary to lay again the very foundations of their faith. What could be more basic than repentance and faith? What is a Christian but someone who has repented from sin, and indeed from *dead works*, and has turned in faith to the Lord Jesus? If we fall far enough down the long backward slope, the point will be reached when we become unsure of where we stand with God. If you ask such a person whether he is a Christian, he will answer; 'I used to think so, but now I'm not so sure'. He has become vague and uncertain about the gospel itself, namely what it means to be right with God. The person who has entered spiritual second childhood will be unsure about where he stands before God for this precise reason: he has forgotten the rudiments of

Christianity. This should alert us to the danger of backsliding. The author's words in 6: 4-6 are very striking:

> For it is impossible for those who were once enlightened, and have tasted the heavenly gift, and have become partakers of the Holy Spirit, and have tasted the good word of God and the powers of the age to come, if they fall away, to renew them again to repentance, since they crucify again for themselves the Son of God, and put Him to an open shame.

These verses describe people who profess Christianity, fall away, and never return to the faith they once professed. No doubt they look back on the time when they claimed to be Christians, and pass it off as a phase which they once went through. How can we tell the difference between people like that on the one hand and the backsliding Christian on the other? Both make a promising start, and both slip back. The only difference is that the backslider returns. If you and I are no longer where we once were, we must think hard. Should we not return to the Lord? We need something like a second conversion. We must turn away from sin, and turn in faith to a pardoning God. Would it not be so much better, however, to ensure that we never fall away in the first place? How is your memory? Have you kept a tight grip on Christian truth?

Another symptom of spiritual second childhood is poor digestion. Children often frustrate their parents very much with their unwillingness to eat good food. Older people are sometimes unable to digest things they once enjoyed. They have lost their healthy appetite. This was the condition of the readers of this epistle. Verse 12 says that they had *come to need milk*. At one time it had been different. Their spiritual appetite had been robust. Now they could only cope with food they could easily digest.

Let us test ourselves at this point. What is our attitude to spiritual food? Some people betray a very sickly appetite indeed. They don't approach Bible Study with enthusiasm. They play listlessly, like a child, picking half-heartedly at his dinner. They find preaching indigestible. This can be the fault of the preacher, but many believers resemble baby birds. Their food must be digested by someone else first. Unless it's light, and in small amounts, they will not tolerate it. Such people often exert pressure in churches to dilute the preaching ministry. The problem is their own digestive systems. Another revealing aspect can be a person's response to Christian company. When people are talking about spiritual things, the backslider will feel uneasy, and will frequently try to turn the conversation to something less searching. It is unnatural for an adult to want nothing but baby food. How do we measure up?

A further symptom is poor co-ordination. Many small children find walking difficult. Older people find the same, and things that they did with ease become a frustrating trial of patience. Ordinary actions like boiling kettles or opening tins become dangerous. The spiritual equivalent is in verse 13. There are those who become *unskilled in the word of righteousness*. Their use of God's Word is clumsy. There are wide gaps in their knowledge. They get things out of scriptural balance. They neglect major matters and blow up unimportant things into bigger things. In particular, they cannot discern good and evil. This does not mean that they cannot tell right from wrong, but they cannot discern good doctrine from bad. Their knowledge of the Word of God is so limited that they are unable to apply it in practical situations.

The word *exercise* in verse 14 is helpful here. Muscles that are not used become useless. The backslider neglects to employ his spiritual faculties, and they shrivel up. The parallel is clear: the person who studies the Word of God will handle it skilfully. The person who does not will not. Are you taking regular exercise?

The antidote to backsliding

A backsliding Christian is a contradiction. The essence of discipleship is discipline, but this is what is absent in the life of the backslider. He claims to follow Jesus, but when Jesus moves on, he falls behind. Even if we sense this it is not easy to prevent, we must not feel superior, as if we could not backslide. If great men and women of the Bible have done so, who is to say that we will not? *Do not be haughty, but fear!* (Romans 11:20).

If we are to guard against backsliding, the first essential is to recognise that at the heart of the problem is a conflict of loyalties. These Jewish believers were pulled in opposite directions. They had reached a point in their Christian experience where they had to make a choice. If Jesus truly was the high priest who superseded all the high priests of Aaron's line, then Judaism was redundant. How tempting it was to cling to the past. Jewish roots, and Jewish family connections exerted a powerful tug. They knew the old and familiar things would have to be left behind if they were going to follow Jesus. It is human, but tragic. They thought that they were going to lose something. In fact they had the opportunity to gain everything. In Christ they had a better prophet than Moses, a better priest than Aaron, and a better sacrifice than all the lambs in Palestine.

No one loses by following Jesus decidedly and fervently. The Son of God himself promised that anyone who suffered for his sake would be richly compensated:

Assuredly, I say to you, there is no one who has left house or brothers or sisters or father or mother or wife or children or lands, for My sake and the gospel's, who shall not receive a hundredfold now in this time — houses and brothers and sisters and mothers and children and lands, with persecutions — and in the age to come, eternal life (Mark 10:29-30).

Jesus, himself, is worth more than anything else could ever be. Are you an unbeliever? Don't believe the nonsense that you will lose out if you surrender to Jesus. You will not miss the things that you leave behind for his sake. Like Paul, you will regard them as rubbish (See Philippians 3:4-9). Are you a wobbly Christian, wondering whether the price of real discipleship is too high? Fix your mind on Jesus. Let him occupy his rightful place in your thoughts. Seek him continually. Try to ensure that every time of prayer, every Bible reading, every sermon and attendance at the Lord's Table becomes an encounter with the living Christ. Seek him for continued pardon, and grace for daily living. Never lose the sense that without him you can do nothing. Follow after him with single-minded determination.

13

CHRISTIAN BASICS

Please read Hebrews 6:1-3

Introduction

Our section begins with a challenge: *let us go on to perfection!* That word *perfection* can mislead us. It translates a Greek word that means completion or maturity. The writer is not exhorting us to reach a state of sinlessness. No one this side of heaven is entirely free of sin. The writer, however, is urging us to make progress. The first readers of this letter had fallen into a state of spiritual second childhood. No builder would ever lay a foundation, only to dig it up and lay it all over again, yet the condition of these believers was like that.

The author helps us greatly here by describing the foundation. We may be Christians who need to heed the challenge to move on. Others may not even have started to build. In either case, it will help us immensely to consider *the elementary principles of Christ.* Verses 1-3 mention six things which teach us Christian basics.

1. Repentance

Repentance is fundamental to Christianity. The call to repent occurs again and again in the New Testament. John the Baptist urged his hearers to *repent, for the kingdom of heaven is at hand!* (Matthew 3:2). The Lord Jesus himself issued the same call. He was a preacher of repentance. On the day of Pentecost, the apostle Peter's preaching brought many people to see their terrible guilt in sending Jesus to his death. He told them that remission of sins was available, but only if they would repent (Acts 2:38). Today, many people are confused about repentance. The Roman Catholic Church teaches that there is a sacrament called penance, which requires a special ceremony, and the services of a clergyman. This is not so. Repentance is very straightforward. It means that we turn away from something. We repudiate it. We put it behind us for ever. We change direction. Repentance begins with a change of heart. When we see things in a new way we realise that a break with the past is necessary. In short, repentance is a complete turn around, firstly in our outlook, and then in our whole lives.

What must we put behind us? The answer given in verse 1 is *dead works* (see also 9:14). Why did the author choose this expression, instead of saying 'repentance from sin'? It is because he wished to cover as much as possible. No one would say publicly that sin is a good thing. Everyone is opposed to sin! (People, however, often redefine it to suit themselves). Be assured of this. We are indeed to repent of sin. Every form of wrongdoing offends the Almighty. Nevertheless, there are other things besides blatant sins that we must shun. *Dead works* include much more. Firstly, all human beings are by nature *dead in trespasses and sins* (Ephesians 2:1; Colossians 2:13). Until the grace of God changes men and women, every thought and activity of each member of the human species, springs from a dead heart. All our words and deeds have the taint of death upon them, and not merely those that are obviously wicked. Our actions do not flow from the life within us, for there is none. They are the consequence of a decayed moral nature. Isaiah had this in mind when he said that even *our righteousnesses are like filthy rags* (Isaiah 64:6). The good deeds that we are proud of come from inward pollution, as well as the things that shame us. This applies to a great deal of religious activity. In fact, much religious behaviour offends God (see Isaiah 1:10-15). Religious works are often as dead as any other kind. Some people need to repent of their churchgoing, their prayers, charity and other observances.

Further, the behaviour of an unconverted person amounts to *dead works* because it results in death. *The wages of sin is death* (Romans 6:23). God ensures that each one receives what he deserves. We all deserve punishment. We have earned everlasting punishment because sin characterises our lives from first to last. *There is a way which seems right to a man, but its end is the way of death* (Proverbs 14:12). Repentance is not just a moral duty, but plain common sense. It is dangerous to go on as we are. Who knows when the time will come to settle accounts with his God? Destruction awaits the person who will not repent. Do we know anything of repentance? Have we turned away from dead works? No one is a Christian unless he has done so.

2. Faith

Faith is fundamental to Christianity. Christians are believers. Furthermore, faith always accompanies repentance. In Acts 20:21 Paul defined the gospel as *repentance toward God, and faith in our Lord Jesus Christ*. Faith is the positive aspect that balances the negative aspect of repentance. If repentance involves turning away from sin, faith involves turning to God. In verse 1 faith is described as *faith towards God*. The God of the Bible has revealed himself only through Christ. As we have seen, the author makes this clear in 1:2. God is not silent, indeed, he has never been silent. The God who once took pity on human ignorance by revealing himself through the prophets had given a much more complete revelation of himself through his Son. We may know all that we need to know of God by considering the Son through whom he speaks. Moreover, we must not only pay close attention to all that God says through his Son. The author would also have us understand that God's Son is also his appointed High Priest who is *able to save to the uttermost those who come to God through him* (7:25).

At the same time, we need to recognise that the author has more in mind than saving faith. In Chapter 11 he defines faith as *the substance of things hoped for, the evidence of things not seen* (11:1). Faith is the ability to see beyond the world that we perceive through our physical senses and to recognise that the unseen realities deserve our attention. To the man of faith, the things that God has promised are even more real and substantial than the transient realities of a world that is passing away. In Chapter 11 we encounter a number of figures from the Old Testament who all exhibited this kind of faith. The first people to read this epistle had acted in the same way. They had made the promises of God the main focus of their lives, convinced that the future held much greater rewards than the present because they were convinced that God would stand by his word. It was in this very area that the author was concerned about his readers. In the recent past they had been able to endure persecution and cope with malicious damage to their property because these things seemed trifling compared with the glory that awaited them but now the author feared that their grip on the unseen world was no longer as secure as it had been.

3. Baptisms

This word is rather puzzling. It does not translate the normal Greek for 'baptism' in the New Testament, but one that can mean 'washings' or 'ablutions'. It is also plural. Why baptisms and not baptism? Several suggestions have been put forward, one being that new converts learned that Christian baptism had replaced the many Jewish ritual washings. The old washings of Judaism no longer mattered; a single baptism was the mark of the person converted to Christ. The experience of certain believers in Ephesus is an example. The baptism which John the Baptist taught was not enough (see Acts 19:1–5).

Note the order here. The New Testament writers always closely associated baptism with the beginning of the Christian life. Peter told his hearers at Pentecost to repent and be baptised (Acts 2:38). Paul told the jailer at Philippi to believe. When he had done so, Paul baptised him (Acts 16:33). Does this mean that baptism is essential for salvation? Do only baptised persons go to heaven? Emphatically not! If that were so, the dying thief at Calvary could only go to Paradise if he were baptised before his death. There are baptised unbelievers and unbaptised believers. What then is the place of baptism? Look at Jesus' command to his disciples in Matthew 28:19-20:

> Go therefore and make disciples of all the nations, baptising them in the name of the Father and of the Son and of the Holy Spirit, teaching them to observe all things that I have commanded you; and lo, I am with you always, even to the end of the age. Amen.

Those who become disciples are to be baptised as part of that discipleship. Christ commands it of his followers. This is fitting, for it is an eloquent testimony of repentance and faith. The symbolism is graphic. Burial in a watery grave speaks of the old life, now left behind. Rising from the water speaks of the new life of faith and service. In recent years some ministers have been in the habit of inviting people to go forward to the front of their churches at evangelistic services. They sometimes say that this is not so much that they might be converted, but rather as a means of testifying publicly that they have been. According to Scripture however, when someone wishes to testify that he has repented of dead works and come to faith in Christ, he is to be baptised.

4. Laying on of hands

Some argue that this statement gives authority for the practice of 'confirmation'. However, this verse mentions laying on of hands and no more. The Bible does not have one clear example of confirmation anywhere. Even so, though it is not hard to say what this statement does not mean, it is not at all easy to decide what it does mean. The laying on of hands in the New Testament church accompanied a variety of things: the ordination of church officers and healing the sick. Perhaps it is connected with Acts 8:17 where we read that the apostles laid hands on Samaritan believers who then received the Holy Spirit. Certainly, every new believer receives the Spirit of God. It may be the case, though we cannot be certain, that the laying on of hands was intended to symbolise the believer's reception of the Holy Spirit, a practice which has since died out.

5 and 6. Resurrection of the dead and eternal judgement

These two things go together. Everyone will die one day. Look at the words of Jesus in John 5:28-29:

> Do not marvel at this; for the hour is coming in which all who are in the graves will hear His voice and come forth – those who have done good, to the resurrection of life, and those who have done evil, to the resurrection of condemnation.

The Christian is aware that a judgement awaits, and that it will have eternal consequences. The verdict pronounced on every human soul by the Son of God will be fixed and unalterable. Eternal life awaits those who believe, and eternal damnation those who do not. The alternatives are in direct contrast to one another. Some are saved for ever, others are damned for ever. Many of us, at our conversion, woke up to the reality of eternal judgement. To know our days are numbered is a great incentive to gain a heart of wisdom (see Psalm 90:12). The approaching end gives an added reality to everything. Repentance is all the more urgent when we realise that a righteous judge is waiting at the end of life's journey. Few people cry to God for the gift of faith like those who know that without it they are destined for eternal ruin.

Moreover, the believer who is conscious that time is short has an excellent incentive to get things in proportion. What really matters in life? There is not much time left in which to accomplish something for the Kingdom of God (see John 9:4). Are we putting our efforts into something lasting, or do we devote our resources and energies to something that will end one day soon. What have I done that will stand for eternity? At this point we would do well to consider the apostle Paul's words in 1 Corinthians 3:11-15:

> For no other foundation can anyone lay than that which is laid, which is Jesus Christ. Now if anyone builds on this foundation with gold, silver, precious stones, wood, hay, straw, each one's work will become manifest; for the Day will declare it, because it will be revealed by fire; and the fire will test each one's work, of what sort it is. If anyone's work, which he has built on it, endures, he will receive a reward. If anyone's work is burned, he will suffer loss; but he himself will be saved, yet so as through fire.

Whatever point we have reached on life's journey, these are sobering words. Only one foundation will stand secure when the world itself is dissolved. Have we started to build on it? Have we repented of sin, and turned in faith to Christ? If not, the whole elaborate structure that we have erected will be no more use than a house of cards. On the other hand, if we have built for eternity on the bedrock of Jesus' mercy, what then? Have we anything to show for it? Let us go on to maturity!

> Therefore, since all these things will be dissolved, what manner of persons ought you to be in holy conduct and godliness, looking for and hastening the coming of the day of God, because of which the heavens will be dissolved, being on fire, and the elements will melt with fervent heat? (2 Peter 3:11-12)

14

A TRAGIC IMPOSSIBILITY

Please read Hebrews 6:4-8

What these verses appear to teach

These verses can be very disturbing to a thoughtful reader. The writer intends us to take them seriously. They describe people in deep trouble. They are a warning to all who read the epistle, whether in the first century or today. We learn from these verses the shocking truth that it is impossible to renew some people *to repentance*.

Who are these people? Many have concluded that they are Christians. At first sight the words of the passage appear to support this view. They are *enlightened*, have *tasted the heavenly gift* and experience in some sense the work of the Holy Spirit (4). Furthermore, they *have tasted the good word of God, and the powers of the age to come* (5). Christians can be filled with anxiety when they first read this passage. It seems to say that a converted person may fall so far that recovery becomes impossible. The sensitive Christian who knows how easily he sins may begin to feel very insecure at this point. Can he be certain that he will go on to the end of the course? Furthermore, there are Christian groups that teach that the believer may indeed fall from grace. According to them, he may lose his salvation. This is not a view that only a few Christians hold. Sooner or later, most of us will encounter people who think along these lines. They usually appeal to these verses in particular to support their teaching.

If these people have understood this passage correctly, certain things inevitably follow. First of all, it introduces an element of uncertainty into the Christian life. The outcome is always in doubt. Will I go to heaven? If it all depends on my performance it is impossible to have any assurance of salvation. The Christian who cannot know from one day to the next whether he will persevere in the favour of God will be very worried. Secondly, we find ourselves asking some questions about God himself. If he abandons the people whom he adopts as his sons and daughters, the Almighty is a short-term foster parent, and a fickle one at that. Are we to conclude that God cannot keep his property safe? Does he protect believers against the wiles of Satan, but not against their own weakness? Let us be in no doubt; if a truly converted person may lose his salvation, our view of both the gospel and of God himself will have to change.

What do these verses teach?

These verses do not teach that Christians can cease to be Christians. There are many passages in the Bible that make it clear that a believer's place in the love of God is secure. *For the LORD loves justice, and does not forsake His saints; they are preserved forever, but the descendants of the wicked shall be cut off* (Psalm 37:28). (See also John 10:28-29; Ephesians 1:13-14; 1 Peter 1:4-5; Romans 8:29-30). But in that case, whom is the writer describing in vv.4–6? The pronouns give us a clue; they indicate a change of emphasis. In verses 1-3 the author uses inclusive language: *us* and *we*. From verse 4 to verse 8 he uses words like *they* and *those*. Then, from verse 9 onwards, the language is personal once more: **we** *are confident of better* *things concerning* **you.** The author's use of words suggests that he was not necessarily assuming that his readers were in the condition that he was warning against.

Nevertheless, the people whom he mentions in verses 4-6 are not complete unbelievers who know nothing of the Christian faith. They are people with spiritual advantages. They have privileges that many do not share. First of all, we are told that they have been *enlightened* (4). Scholars in the Middle Ages regarded this as a reference to baptism. (At that time, new candidates were not baptised until they had been through a period of instruction). The crucial question is whether or not it means conversion. It is true that the eyes of every believer have been opened to the truth as it is in Jesus. Even so, not everyone who is enlightened is saved. Conversion is more than enlightenment. Speaking of his own conversion, the apostle Paul once said that he was not disobedient to the heavenly vision (Acts 26:19). It began with an experience of enlightenment, but Paul did not stop there. He brought his life into line with it. Sadly, there are people who realise that they ought to follow Christ, but resist.

The word *tasted* (4) is interesting. It is not intended to portray something that is merely superficial, as though these people have tasted but have not swallowed! These people evidently have a real experience, but are all experiences of God adequate? They have tasted *the heavenly gift.* But what can this be? Salvation itself is a gift. (If it were not, no one would ever be saved, for it cannot be earned). The Holy Spirit is also given to believers. The greatest of God's gifts to men, however, is the Lord Jesus Christ. In John 4:10, in conversation with the woman at the well, Jesus referred to himself in precisely that way. Some people share in that gift in a limited way. They claim to follow Jesus, give assent to the truths of Christianity, and move in Christian circles. They come under Christian influence, and may well appear to be believers. They have more of Christ than an

atheist or heathen, but they still do not have saving faith.
Another thing that they have tasted is *the good word of God*
(5). True preaching is no ordinary thing. It should not surprise
us when it affects people. Nevertheless, preaching should do
more than stir us, frighten us, move us to tears and even prompt
us to amend our lifestyles. There is more to salvation than an
emotional crisis.

What does *the powers of the age to come* (5) mean? We
would be wrong to suppose that this refers to the distant future.
The Jews of the first century commonly divided time into two
periods: 'these days', and 'the age of Messiah'. When we looked
at chapter 1 we saw that Christians live in a transitional period,
'the end of these days', or 'the last days'. The age of Messiah is
not yet with us in its fullness, but it has begun. The power of
God is undoubtedly at work in the world. Some have tasted it.
In verse 4 this is stated even more strongly. We are told that
some people *have become partakers of the Holy Spirit.* Surely
people like that must be Christians? Did not Paul say *if any
man does not have the Spirit of Christ, he is not His* (Romans
8:9)? We must grasp here that spiritual power does not guarantee
the status of the person who employs it. Look at Jesus' words
in Matthew 7:21–23 concerning the final judgement,

> Not everyone who says to Me, 'Lord, Lord', shall enter
> the kingdom of heaven, but he who does the will of My
> Father in heaven. Many will say to Me in that day, 'Lord,
> Lord, have we not prophesied in Your name, cast out
> demons in Your name, and done many wonders in Your
> name?' And then I will declare to them, 'I never knew
> you; depart from Me, you who practice lawlessness.'

These are sobering words. The Spirit of God occasionally uses
people as his instruments who are not right with God. Judas
the traitor worked genuine miracles. God looks for more than

gifts when he assesses the state of our hearts. Balaam and Saul prophesied but their hearts were rotten. Gifts say nothing about character, and that is the great indicator of the Holy Spirit's presence in a human life. When he takes up residence in the heart, holiness begins to pervade the character.

Verse 6 tells us that these people *fall away*. They do not fall away from salvation for they were never saved in the first place. There is no doubt that they had come a long way, and had experienced more of God than many, but they still fell short. The background to this epistle will help us at this point. Its first readers were ethnic Jews. They had made a promising start, but had begun to waver. Their difficulty was that they had begun to grasp just how demanding commitment to Christ can be. It involves a clean break with the past, in their case, their Jewish past. This explains the challenge in verse 1 *let us go on to perfection*. This does not mean that a Christian can reach a state of sinless perfection in this life. Some Christians argue that such a thing is taught in the Bible. At any rate, it is not taught in Hebrews. The whole context of this part of the epistle is a debate about priesthood. It contrasts an imperfect priesthood, that of Aaron, with one that is perfect, namely that of Christ. Chapter 7:11 sums this up beautifully,

> Therefore, if perfection were through the Levitical priesthood (for under it the people received the law), what further need was there that another priest should rise according to the order of Melchizedek, and not be called according to the order of Aaron?

Thus, when the author told his readers to go on to perfection, he was challenging them to shake off their ancestral attachment to outmoded Jewish forms of worship that were only ever meant to be preparatory. These believers had reached a point where faith in Christ was becoming costly. As ethnic Jews, living in a Jewish environment, they faced a decisive choice. They could face up to the implications of their Christian profession. If Jesus truly is the only High Priest who can bring us to God, then they must follow him and accept the consequences. Alternatively, they could try to cling to the priesthood of Aaron, knowing that this would guarantee a quiet life. If they still lived the outward life of Jews, hostility would pass them by. Verse 6 tells us what this would actually mean. It would be crucifying *the Son of God* afresh. Does that seem strong language? It is no more than the truth. A person says that his only hope of salvation is Christ, and that he has no other confidence. The same person says later that he means to go on placing his trust in the old way of life that he claimed to have left behind. This means that he has, in effect, denied the faith that he once professed. Even today, there are still people who do the same. Their profession of faith is a temporary phase. They 'put their hands to the plough' and then turn back, and prove in so doing that they are not fit for the kingdom of God. Their position is serious. It is impossible to renew them to repentance! Remember, repentance is a change of heart and mind. We are describing people who knowingly and deliberately go back on the Christianity that they once claimed to embrace.

The proof of genuineness is perseverance. This is the point of the illustration in verses 7-8. Two plots of soil are watered by the rain. One produces a crop, the other produces nothing but weeds. Two people hear of the claims of Christ. They both experience the Holy Spirit's work. Both make a start. Time passes; one falters and stagnates, the other makes progress. Let us not forget that Christian growth does not always go on at a uniform rate. We sustain our temporary reverses, we have our failures. Our weakness leads us again and again to seek restoration from our great High Priest. A true believer may 'backslide'. This is what makes the lesson of this passage so vital. On the face of it, a backslider will look very similar to the person mentioned here. How can he prove that his faith was not temporary? He must return to consistent discipleship. In any case, every Christian knows the sad reality of backsliding. We simply vary in the extent to which we regress. Days, months, or years, the challenge is the same. We cannot live on past experience. Let us go on!

Summary of verses 4-8

We began our study of this section by noting that these words can have an unsettling effect on the reader. No one should dismiss them lightly for while they do not contradict the impressive array of scriptures that teach that all of Christ's people are saved forever, they issue a solemn warning that some profess faith in Christ who subsequently fall away, never to be restored. There is such a thing as counterfeit Christianity. Some people deceive themselves and others into thinking that they are genuine followers of Jesus. They are not found out until a period of time has passed and their false claims are exposed when they fail to endure testing. In the meantime, they give a passable imitation of a true Christian. John Bunyan had such a person in mind in his closing section of the first part of *Pilgrim's Progress*. A man called Ignorance had followed Christian and Hopeful all the way to the entrance to the Celestial City, only to be refused admittance. 'Then I saw that there was a way to hell, even from the gates of heaven, as well as from the City of Destruction.' The author felt that his first readers needed to hear this grim warning because they were no longer as spiritually responsive as they had once been (5:12-14). Some professing Christians today also need to pause and take stock. Perhaps we no longer follow Jesus as we once did. What does this mean? Does it not indicate that we need to return to our *first love*, to *repent and do the first works* (Revelation 2:4, 5)? Equally, we may have to face up to the disturbing possibility that we were never truly converted at all and need to seek the mercy of God for the very first time.

Therefore let him who thinks he stands take heed lest he fall (1 Corinthians 10:12). Therefore, brethren, be even more diligent to make your call and election sure, for if you do these things you will never stumble (2 Peter 1:10).

15
SURE AND STEADFAST

Please read Hebrews 6:9-20

Introduction

The theme of these verses is hope. Hope is not something speculative. In everyday English, when we say that we 'hope' something will happen, we mean that we would like things to turn out in a certain way but are not confident that they will. For the writers of the New Testament, however, hope and confidence were the same thing. This hope is more than mere optimism. Verse 19 compares it to an anchor fixed in the seabed, solid and immovable, 'sure and steadfast'. What a contrast with the preceding verses! In verses 4-6 we read about people who live in a way that makes us wonder if they are Christians at all. It is likely that the first readers of this epistle were troubled as they read these words. They had begun well, but after a time their discipleship had become shaky. Sensitive spirits among them were probably wondering whether they fitted that sombre description of people who fall away and cannot be renewed to repentance. The author has words of comfort for them. In verse 9 he addresses them as his *beloved*, he is convinced that his readers really were Christians. We do well to examine his thinking, for we can apply it to our own situation. Are we Christians? Can we produce convincing evidence, or do we delude ourselves? Is any question, in the entire world, more important than this?

Hope is strengthened by diligence

Verse 10 tells us something about the character of those Hebrew believers. In the past they had served their fellow Christians, and even though their discipleship was not as consistent as it had been at the beginning, they continued to show kindness to the *saints*. In the first century this needed courage. If you identified with Christians and showed in various ways that you were on their side, people took notice. It made you conspicuous. The author assured his readers that God would not be so churlish as to overlook this. We must never imagine that God is indifferent to our conduct. When believers do well, their Father notes it with approval. Indeed, it thrills his heart! The letters to the seven churches in Revelation (Revelation 2:1-3:22) contain a phrase that occurs again and again. The risen Christ says to each one: *I know your works.* These words tolled like a bell in the ears of careless and hypocritical Christians, but were full of gentle reassurance to the persecuted church at Smyrna, and the faithful church at Philadelphia. God neither forgets our obedience, nor ignores our achievements.

We need not be alarmed at this point. Although there are people who say that God accepts us because of what we do, the author is not one of them! Proud human beings like to think that they can contribute to their salvation, but the unanimous verdict of the Bible is that they cannot earn or buy the favour of God. Because we sin, our best efforts to merit God's acceptance are useless. God saves people because of free grace and for no other reason. Nevertheless, our behaviour as believers matters. We must not confuse the 'ground' of our salvation with the 'evidence' for it. In verse 9 we read that the kind acts of the Hebrews were *things that accompany salvation.* Salvation is never solitary. It is always accompanied by good deeds. If we grasp the connection between salvation and the things that accompany it, this will protect us from two fatal errors. The first error is the idea that our actions buy God's favour. Be in no doubt: good deeds do not merit salvation, they come with it. At the same time let us never imagine that a saved person will not behave well. If the accompaniments are not there, we are entitled to wonder about salvation itself. The phrase *labour of love* in verse 10 is most helpful. What is the Christian's motive for holy living? Is it the desire to win salvation? Emphatically not! He does what he does out of love for the person who has saved him.

This becomes intensely practical when we interview people for church membership. Is there a conversion story? More to the point, is there evidence that conversion has taken place? If the accompaniments are present, so is salvation. Furthermore, every Christian must look at himself in this way too. *Full assurance* is partly a product of *diligence* (11). If, as we examine our lives, we can see that our labour provides consistent and growing evidence of our love for Christ, our hope in the favour of God will strengthen. Inconsistent disciples do not usually enjoy their Christianity. Satan has countless opportunities to insinuate that real Christians do not act as they do. The believer who makes progress will be far more happy in his God. He can provide solid proof that his faith is more than just an illusion.

The example of Abraham's hope

It is always an incentive to our endeavours to have someone that we can look up to. (One sad feature of modern life is that cynicism has robbed our young people of heroes). Verse 12 told the Hebrews that if they were sluggish, they would be unworthy of their ancestors, who inherited the promises. In most normal situations, no-one inherits the property of another unless he has a right to it. You don't acquire the property of a perfect stranger, but of a loved one who has died. So how do we prove that we have a right to heaven? Certainly not by being sluggish. That will only raise doubts, both in our minds, and in others. We must persevere! There are many whose *faith and patience* we could imitate, (chapter 11 contains a stirring list), but the verses before us invite us to concentrate on Abraham.

Verse 15 speaks of patient endurance. This is no exaggeration in Abraham's case. God promised him that all the nations of the earth would be blessed through his offspring. Twenty-five years passed between the promise and the birth of Isaac. Even as we contemplate this impressive record, we must not suppose that Abraham was free from ordinary human frailty. His faith in God's promise went through some severe trials. At one stage he became the father of an illegitimate son, Ishmael, by his wife's maid Hagar, in an attempt to hurry things along. On another occasion he despaired enough to consider making out a will in favour of Eliezer of Damascus, his nearest male relative. Abraham was not perfect, one of those individuals whose unending success depresses us. Like us, he knew his reverses. Nevertheless, he made progress. His faith surmounted the obstacles. Undoubtedly the greatest of these was the incident on Mount Moriah (see Genesis 22:1-19). When his son, Isaac, was born the temptation to rest his hope in the boy would be very strong. Every believing person faces the same challenge. Human nature prefers to rely on God's blessings rather than on God himself. Abraham triumphed because, in the course of his long experience, he had learned that God was reliable. Even if Isaac lay dead on the altar, and that both he and Sarah his wife were long past the age of child-bearing, God would keep his promise. God cannot lie. This puts perseverance in its proper perspective. Abraham's patience is remarkable, and we do well to copy it, but it is only what God expects. If, at some stage, Abraham had given up in disgust, he would have accused God of lying. Do we grasp this? When, in our moments of despair we feel like giving it all up, do we realise what we are doing? Are we really going to say that God is not worthy of our trust?

Christian hope has a worthy object

Abraham's obedience on this occasion prompted the Almighty to swear the oath (see Genesis 22:17) recorded in verse 14. This is amazing. It is a sad fact that oaths are required in every-day life because human promises are unreliable. God, how-ever, *is not a man that He should lie* (Numbers 23:19). Why should someone who is the truth need to guarantee his conduct? Nevertheless, for the sake of Abraham his friend, the Lord of heaven and earth confirmed his earlier promise with a solemn pledge. Moreover, this is not the only oath that he has sworn. In verse 17 we are told of another oath that he made for the *heirs of promise*. In short, God made it for the sake of all believers, including you and me. Our God is very gracious! His bare word ought to be enough to convince anybody, and yet he is so generous that he is willing to go a step further. In effect he has pledged himself twice. Now there can be no possible doubt that *his counsel* (17) is immutable. His word is depend-able. His yes is yes, and his no is no!

The oath in question was mentioned in 5:6. (Remember that the main subject of these middle chapters of Hebrews is the High Priesthood of Christ. We now return to it after a digression). The Almighty declares to Messiah that he is a perpetual High Priest *according to the order of Melchizedek*. This follows the earlier declaration in 5:5 that he was the only begotten of God. The writer now puts together these two facts about Christ and describes them in 6:18 as *two immutable things in which it is impossible for God to lie*. He does not intend them only for Messiah's benefit but also to provide believers with *strong consolation*. A double guarantee from the Almighty should provide all the reassurance anyone could ever want.

Why should believers be strengthened by the knowledge that Jesus is a High Priest for ever? Verses 18 and 19 describe people fleeing for refuge, who place their hope in an anchor. We are like ships at sea. Danger threatens on every side. The ocean itself is turbulent, and we have to contend with storms and the dangers of a rock-bound coast. How long can the fragile, leaky little vessel stay afloat? Will it founder? Will it be hurled to destruction on a reef? This is an extraordinarily vivid picture of the Christian life. We can ride out the storm in perfect safety, but only because an immovable anchor fastens us securely to bedrock. Christians have exactly that! If you are not a Christian, pause for a moment and think about your situation. You have no security worthy of the name; you are like a small boat adrift in a hurricane.

Why is the Christian's anchor so firm? It is because it is fixed where nothing can dislodge it, *behind the veil*. At first sight, this might seem rather strange. We are being asked to think of the inner sanctuary of the temple, the most holy place, where God is to be found. The anchor of the soul is placed there. This is only a picture of something far grander. Verse 20 portrays Jesus as one of the priests of Israel, going through the veil into the presence of God. In fact, he has accomplished something still more wonderful, having gone into God's presence as our representative, our *forerunner*. The veil no longer exists, the barriers are down. Jesus himself is the anchor! Chapter 5:6 tells us that he is priest *forever*. The priests of Aaron's line entered the most holy place and then left it for another year. They came and went. Jesus has entered God's presence and will never leave it. Our hope is fixed, because the anchor is fixed, permanently! Furthermore, he is our *forerunner*. Again this marks a difference between Jesus and the priests of Israel. The priests went behind the veil, and no-one followed. Jesus has entered the presence of God as the first of a vast company. Why can the believer be sure of heaven? First of all, because Jesus has gone first to prepare the way, and secondly we are certain to follow since God has guaranteed that Jesus' presence there is permanent, and all his people will follow him into heaven.

In conclusion two things are vital if our hope is to be sure and steadfast. We must live out the Christian life with diligence! At the same time, since we are so fickle and unstable, how can we be confident that we shall persevere? Only by remembering the promises of the God who cannot lie, namely that Christ will never cease to be his people's priest, and their guarantee of eternal safety. With such an anchor, who could fail? In what do you place your hope? Are your moorings secure?

16
ACCORDING TO THE ORDER OF MELCHIZEDEK

Please read Hebrews 7:1-28

Introduction

One of the great themes of this epistle is Jesus, the perpetual High Priest of his people. This theme confronted the first recipients of this letter with a dilemma. If Jesus truly is a High Priest, what of their ancestral religion? Did their commitment to Jesus require them to turn their backs on something that God himself had given? It is difficult for us to appreciate how much the priesthood meant to Jews of the first century. The high priest, in particular, was the awesome embodiment of the whole system. The requirements for selection to this position were rigorous. It was not enough to be an Israelite. It was an hereditary post, confined to a single family. This privileged individual wore the name of God on his mitre, and he alone out of the entire nation, could enter the most holy place in the temple, once a year on the Day of Atonement.

The amazing claim of this epistle was that there was now a better High Priest, and that the Old Testament Scriptures proved this fact. Modern Christians sometimes find it difficult to understand the relevance of the Old Testament Scriptures. We can see why they would matter to converts from first century Judaism, but what bearing do they have on our lives today? Ever since the beginning, Christianity has had to fight against a tendency to slip back into a Jewish mould. Little by little, ritual and formality threaten to replace the simplicity of the early days. It was not long before the old idea reasserted itself that the people of God needed to be kept at a distance while a special class of priests mediated on their behalf. Moreover the idea of lineage crept in once more, not this time physical descent from the family of Aaron, but the principle of apostolic succession. (In other words, true priests are those who trace their ordination right back to the apostles). On top of all this, a particular bishop began to claim that he and his successors were Pontifex Maximus. (The Pope claims this Latin title, meaning High Priest.) It was not long before church architecture began to reflect this outlook. The pattern of the temple was adopted. Ordinary believers had to keep to one end of a church building, and the priests reserved the holy part for themselves. Today, the Ecumenical movement is increasing in momentum because the idea of Christian unity is powerfully attractive. In particular, it is an attempt to bring about unity with those groups that emphasise the idea that real Christianity is priestly. Must we succumb to the pressure? Do we need holy people, with a holy anointing, to do holy things on our behalf, in the holy part of holy buildings, or can we approach God ourselves? It is vitally important that we understand something at this point. This is not a debate between those who have priests and those who do not. Evangelical Christians do have a High Priest!

Melchizedek the prototype

Verses 1-10 look back to events recorded in Genesis 14. The patriarch Abraham had become involved in a war between an alliance of four kings led by Chedorlaomer, king of Elam and another alliance of five kings led by the king of Sodom. Abraham's nephew, Lot, had been taken hostage, so the patriarch led a rescue mission, which overthrew the four kings from the north. When he returned Abraham paid tribute to Melchizedek and received his blessing. This man is an enigmatic figure, mentioned in the Old Testament only here and in Psalm 110. The author to the Hebrews mentions him at this point because he functions like an Old Testament John the Baptist, pointing the way to someone far greater. In the words of verse 3, he was *made like the Son of God*.

The name Melchizedek means *king of righteousness*. He was evidently the king of Salem. Salem refers to Jerusalem, but the word itself means peace. These titles anticipate an even greater King of righteousness and peace. Melchizedek is also *priest of the Most High God* (1). Certainly he behaved as priests do, accepting Abraham's offering and blessing him. The priesthood of Aaron lay in the future at this point, but when it did come about no Israelite could combine the two offices of priest and king. We know nothing of Melchizedek's origins. (Ordinarily the book of Genesis gives detailed genealogical coverage of the background of its heroes). The record is also silent about his death, and any descendants he might have had. His priesthood has not been handed to anyone else, therefore it remains in force.

Abraham, the father of the Jewish race, was rightly revered as a colossus. Moses the lawgiver, David the king, and all the prophets of Israel descended from him. He received the promises of God, and was even called God's friend. Nevertheless, the details of the story point to a remarkable conclusion: Melchizedek was greater than Abraham was. The fact that Abraham deferred to him means that he recognised this; he offered Melchizedek a portion of the spoils of battle, and received his blessing in return. As verse 7 says, this act of blessing tells us something about the relationship of the two men. It also says something about Melchizedek's priesthood in contrast to that of Aaron, who, with his successors, descended from Abraham. If Abraham, their progenitor and father, saw himself as inferior to Melchizedek, then Melchizedek's order of priest-hood must be greater than that of Aaron. So, when the author speaks of Jesus as a High Priest, we are not to picture him as being on a level with all those who were descended from Aaron. When Jesus offered his life as a sacrifice for sin, he fulfilled the prophecy contained in Psalm 110. Like Melchizedek, Messiah is a priest for ever.

A weak and unprofitable priesthood

Verses 11–19 put the Levitical priesthood into its proper perspective. God ordained Old Testament religion but he never intended it to be permanent. Instead, it was provisional and preparatory. Indeed verse 11 suggests that the Jews ought to have known this. Psalm 110 promised a permanent priesthood that was still to come, a priesthood connected with Messiah, and according to the order of Melchizedek. This promise would have been quite superfluous if the Levitical priesthood had been adequate. What could be clearer? God had declared through the Psalmist that, in time, the temporary and unsatisfactory priestly system established in the law of Moses would give way to something better and lasting. Again and again in this epistle we come across the word 'perfect'. Something perfect is to replace something that is imperfect. Why cling to Judaism, when all that it had promised and pointed to had arrived? In Jesus God has given his people a permanent priest. The priests of Israel were nothing more than a picture of better things to come.

The conclusion is inescapable. Once the new and perfect priesthood came, the old and imperfect priesthood, which had never been intended to be a permanent fixture, became redun-dant. Verses 13 and 14 show us that we are dealing with a complete departure from the old system. No one from the tribe of Judah had ever served at the altar, yet Jesus was born to that very tribe. The people received the law through the old covenant, and it had a vital part to play in the purposes of God. Nevertheless, it had served its purpose. In the words of vv.18-19, *the bringing in of a better hope* has the effect of annulling the *former commandment*. Compared with the paganism of the surrounding nations, Judaism stood out like a beacon. Nevertheless, it was always partial and incomplete. When you have arrived at your holiday destination, do you long for the signposts that you passed on the way there? The Jewish converts who first received this letter were in danger of doing something similar. They had Jesus, God's appointed High Priest, yet they hankered after things that could not compare with the blessings that were theirs in Christ, things that were in Paul's phrase, *weak and beggarly elements* (Galatians 4:9). Verse 16 says the old system arose out of a divine commandment, but the one thing it could not give was life. Our new High Priest is endowed with *the power of an endless life*. Why cling to a corpse when there is life to be had?

This is intensely practical. Verse 19 defines how we draw near to God. What is the good of a long and prosperous life if at the end of it we are no nearer to God? We all stand looking over the cliff edge of eternity. Will God accept us? There is no reason why he should. We are sinners. We have all offended him. That is why we need a priest, someone to plead our cause with God, someone to mediate for us. Do not imagine that any Old Testament priest can do this. If the temple still stood in Jerusalem, and the altar still smoked, the author's description would still apply. It would be a weak and unprofitable system. As verse 19 says, *the law made nothing perfect*. It could never reconcile a sinner to God. Only one priest can do that and his name is Jesus.

A perfect priest

The message to those Hebrew believers of long ago was plain. They were not making a sacrifice by loosening their grip on the religion of their childhood, for in Jesus they had something so much better. It is worth noting that some believers think that one day the temple will be rebuilt, and the sacrificial system restored. They base this on their understanding of Ezekiel's vision of a rebuilt temple recorded in Ezekiel 40:1-47:12. Given that Christ has offered the perfect sacrifice for sin, once and for all, and that the sacrifices of the Old Testament era were meant to prefigure his great sacrifice, the point of such a restored sacrificial system is hard to grasp. It would mean returning to the way things were before Christ came. It is probably better to understand Ezekiel's vision as a symbolic way of describing the blessings that restored fellowship with God would bring to his people and the way that he would live among them. Understood in that way, the Christian community is now a *holy temple in the Lord* (Ephesians 2:21).[1] Sadly, there is always a temptation to want to revert to a religion that appeals to the physical senses rather than the simplicity we have in Christ but what spiritual good can be gained from an imposing temple building or for that matter, the architectural splendours of a medieval cathedral? The Christian who has a share in Christ can happily say goodbye to all the priestly paraphernalia of Christendom. What are masses and vestments to the person who has Jesus? Never give way to the propaganda from certain religious bodies that while they have their priests, evangelical Christianity has none. The Christian has a priest worth more than all other priests put together. There is no comparison.

Verses 20 and 21 tell us that the priesthood of Aaron and that of Jesus had different beginnings. God made Jesus a priest by an oath. God has sworn and will not revoke his promise. He did not do this with Aaron's priesthood. Certainly the priesthood came into being through divine enactment, but legislation can always be overturned. If Parliament can change laws then almighty God can dispense with things that have done their work. However, there is nothing temporary about the priesthood of Christ. God has given his word on it. This is a priesthood that will go on for ever.

Verses 22-25 show that the priests of Israel had their limitations. There was a long succession of them because each one was mortal. They grew old and died. They slept with their fathers. The priests of Christendom are no better off. From the humblest curate to the supreme pontiff himself, each one will die. Some of the high priests in Jerusalem, Zadok, Jehoiada and Joshua, were great men. Even so, they cannot help anybody now. They are dead. So it is even with the best of men. How many pastors would love to be able to seek the counsel of some of the great preachers from the past. They cannot do so; these great servants of God are no longer with us. Now consider Jesus. If the world should last another 2,000 years, he will still be there to hear the cries of his children. He lives and cannot die. His people will never be without him. No-one else can *save to the uttermost* (25). As we go through life, the people we depend on are taken from us. Come to Jesus, for he is and will always be the same. His years will not fail.

Why should we take Jesus for our priest? Because none of the others can do what he has done. As verse 27 says, they were sinners themselves. A sinful mediator cannot help me: he too has offended God. He needs a mediator himself! We must learn to place our trust in Jesus. If we do, God will accept us, because he accepts him. He is a *fitting* priest. Look at what verse 26 says about his character: he is *holy, harmless, undefiled, separate from sinners.* Who is like him? Why are people so ready to turn to mere human priests with all their weaknesses, when they could turn instead to the Son, God's perfect priest?

---

[1] For an excellent discussion of the meaning of Ezekiel's vision see the relevant section in C. J. H. Wright, *The Message of Ezekiel*, published by IVP in *The Bible Speaks Today* series.

17

A BETTER COVENANT

Please read Hebrews 8:1-13

Introduction

The central part of this epistle presents Jesus as the High Priest of his people. Here in chapter 8 we come to a new stage in this theme. So far, the author has invited us to compare High Priest with high priest. We have looked at Aaron and his descendants, and seen that Jesus is greater than them all. Verse 1 looks back over the preceding material and reminds us of the wonder of it: *We have such a High Priest.* The high priests of Aaron's line were occasional visitors to the innermost sanctuary of the temple. Jesus has taken up permanent residence at the right hand of God. In verse 2 the author introduces a new comparison. He invites us to compare the ministry of Jesus with that of the Levitical high priests. In the next few chapters we shall learn that Jesus was the mediator of a better covenant, in a better sanctuary, on the basis of a better offering. Every aspect of his ministry was far greater than that of the priests of Israel. In this next section, we shall concentrate on the covenant. Our passage begins, however, with some preliminary remarks about the sanctuary.

The temple in Jerusalem was one of the glories of Israel. The building itself was imposing enough, but first century Jews were struck not so much by the structure but by its purpose.

They saw it as the place where God and men were brought together by the mediation of the high priests. Jews living outside Palestine regarded a visit to the temple as one of life's greatest moments. It was the focus of the religious life of a whole people. The Jews were so emotionally attached to it that even converted Jews would be reluctant to think that it had served its purpose. At this point the author set out to reassure his readers. They were not giving up the temple and getting nothing in return. There was a better sanctuary, the *true tabernacle* (2). In comparison, the temple in Jerusalem was only a *copy and shadow* (5). (Our passage mentions Moses' tabernacle, but the various temples that stood in Jerusalem were stone copies of it. The layout of each temple followed the same pattern originally laid down for the tabernacle.) The ancient tabernacle, and the temples based upon it, were visual aids. The model was glorious but it was only a model. Now the people of God have a High Priest who ministers in the real, heavenly sanctuary.

An obsolete covenant

Verse 4 reminds us that, when Jesus was on earth, he could not have entered the priesthood. This is explained in 7:14. When Moses inaugurated the covenant at Sinai, he did not command men from the tribe of Judah to become priests. The passage before us tells us that this situation was now changing. Look at verse 13. A new covenant had come into force, which rendered the old one obsolete. Soon it would vanish! This suggests that the worship of the temple was still functioning, and that the cataclysm of A.D.70 had not yet taken place. No doubt Jewish believers would feel that the destruction of the temple was the greatest catastrophe possible. They ought to have known better. The Old Testament Scriptures taught that the covenant made at Sinai was never meant to be permanent. God had always intended to supersede it.

At the time of the exodus from Egypt, it was the practice of powerful kings to make treaties with the lesser kings who were their subjects. These treaties would set out in detail the relationship between the Great King and his vassals. The Great King would make certain guarantees. In particular, he would promise his protection. In return, he would impose certain requirements. Subjects would have to pay tribute and disloyalty would be severely punished. The covenant made at Sinai is similar in form to these ancient treaties. Yahweh, the Great King of the whole universe, laid down the conditions that would govern his relationship with his subject nation, Israel. He would be their God, their sovereign and protector. Woe to the enemy who quarrelled with his subjects! Nevertheless, he required something in return: they must obey his Law. This Law included the Ten Commandments which reflected the King's own character, and a host of other regulations governing the national and religious life of the people. The worship of the tabernacle, and the institution of the priesthood were one aspect of this covenant. The covenant included penalties. If Israel did not obey the Law she would incur the Great King's wrath. This throws light on the whole history of Israel. Again and again she *did not continue* in it (9). God sent his prophets to remind the people of the covenant, but the people did not heed their warnings, and as a result Israel was defeated by her enemies, or had to endure the bitterness of exile.

This covenant had its limitations. As verse 7 says, it was not *faultless*. Verse 6 tells us where the problem lay. The new covenant was founded on *better promises*. Clearly, the former covenant was based on ineffective promises. It was a contract between two parties: the King of heaven and the nation of Israel. Divine promises were involved, and human promises too! It broke down when the Israelites who embraced it with enthusiasm at Sinai, did not keep their word. That is why God *found fault* with them (8). The weakness was not in the covenant, for it achieved its purpose. The apostle Paul tells us that God gave the Law to teach us a lesson, namely that we are unable to keep it. It acts as a schoolmaster. It tells us how sinful our hearts are (see Galatians 3:24). Nevertheless, it could never bring people to God, as it depended on fickle human beings. The most detailed agreement will fail if one of the parties involved is incapable of living up to it. Millions of people never learn this lesson. They imagine that they can come to God on the basis of their efforts and achievements. They cannot do it. We ourselves are the problem. The demands of God's Law are too difficult for us.

A better covenant founded on better promises

At this stage in his argument, in vv.8-12, the author includes a quotation from Jeremiah 31:31–34.

> 'Behold, the days are coming, says the LORD, when I will make a new covenant with the house of Israel and with the house of Judah – not according to the covenant that I made with their fathers in the day that I took them by the hand to lead them out of the land of Egypt, My covenant which they broke, though I was a husband to them, says the LORD. But this is the covenant that I will make with the house of Israel, after those days, says the LORD: I will put My law in their minds, and write it on their hearts; and I will be their God, and they shall be My people. No more shall every man teach his neighbour, and every man his brother, saying, "Know the Lord," for they all shall know Me, from the least of them to the greatest of them', says the LORD. For I will forgive their iniquity, and their sin I will remember no more.'

The author introduces this quotation to make an important point, namely that he had not invented the new covenant. It is not

something that we meet for the first time in this letter! Students
of the Old Testament would know that God had already fore-
told it and that the former covenant was not permanent. There
is an important difference between the two covenants: the new
does not share the weakness of the old. It is one-sided. It
consists of promises from God, but requires no human promises in return. It could only break down if God's promises were
unreliable. He has left nothing to chance, however, for he has
founded the covenant solely on what he will do.

The basis of it all is the promise in verse 10 that God will be
a God to his covenant people. There will be a special relationship. Scripture uses many pictorial expressions of this relationship: a king and his subjects, a master and his servants, a
shepherd and his sheep, a father and his children, a husband
and his bride. God and his people belong together. God
intends that he and they will be inseparable. In order to secure
this, God promised through Jeremiah that he would do four
things.

The first promise is found in verse 10. God will put his Law
into their minds, and write his commandments on their hearts.
There was nothing wrong with the Law given at Sinai. It was an
expression of the character of God. It was sublime. The problem lay with the people. This was a law that they could not
keep. Covenants which are based on law have an underlying
principle: *Do this and live.* The sad fact is that no human being
is able to satisfy the requirements laid down in God's holy Law.
No one achieves the reward because no one attains the standard.
Moreover, it is not that we fail through ignorance or misfortune.
At heart we do not want to keep the Law of God. *The heart is
deceitful above all things, and desperately wicked; who can
know it?* (Jeremiah 17:9). But God promises to give us a new
nature. His Law becomes part of us. It is no longer something
'out there', but part of our constitution as redeemed people. It
begins to shape and mould us, and we for our part come to

love it. We are told that if someone is a Christian, old things pass away and everything becomes new (see 2 Corinthians 5:17). Certainly we lose the old hostility to God's Law. People who are not believers resent the idea that God has a right to make demands on them. Believers, however, love to do what pleases him. It is absolutely vital that God promises to do this. None of us would ever be able to change our heart attitude to God and his Law by ourselves.

The second promise concerns a new relationship. God says of his people, *I will be their God and they shall be My people* (10). The idea of belonging is very much to the fore. Martin Luther once said that the essence of religion is in its personal pronouns. While it is wonderfully true to say, *Christ died for the ungodly* (Romans 5:6) it is all the more thrilling to speak, as Paul did, of *the Son of God, who loved me and gave himself for me* (Galatians 2:20). In the same way, for sinful mortals to refer to the Maker of the universe as 'my God' is a privilege so great it sets the senses reeling. There is a sense in which God belongs to us. This is all because of his abundant grace. In his great mercy, he has bound us to him in love. And what could make a believer more secure than to reflect on the equally astonishing fact that God looks on believers as 'my people'? No power on earth or heaven, no combination of forces in existence can threaten the eternal safety of a Christian. There can be no doubt whatever that the Almighty is well able to keep his property safe.

The third promise describes a new experience. God's people will all know him (11). This marks Christianity out from every other religion. It is not enough to know about God, or even to serve him. He is more than an object of worship. He is not remote. He can be known and experienced. Believers relate to him, and enjoy him. They have ties of friendship and family with the Almighty! Knowing God is not a desirable option. It is an absolute necessity. We are told in Matthew 7: 21-23, that when the end of the age comes, Jesus will reject certain people. Those who are banished from his presence forever are those whom he did not know. It is vital to know God. Jesus once said that to know God and his Son is to enjoy eternal life (John 17:3). At the same time, this is an extraordinary privilege, and it is difficult to exaggerate the greatness of it. The good shepherd knows his sheep and they know him (John 10:14). This kind of language is warm and intimate. How can we attain this knowledge? It is God's gift to his covenant people. While we can do nothing to earn or deserve it, the Almighty gives it freely to all who will receive it.

Fourthly, the new covenant also promises a new record (12), complete forgiveness. All our wickedness is forgotten. Believers sometimes find that their attempts to forgive are hampered because their memories are too tenacious. Try as we might, we cannot always shake off the old slights and injuries. It is far from easy to forget what other people have said or done. God does not merely put the past behind him, he completely writes it off. He treats us as if the sins that we mourn never took place. Note that the writer mentions this pardon is in third place, after the promise of a new nature and a new relationship. Even people with a new heart fall into sin. The changes that will make them like Jesus have begun, but are not complete. In the meantime the struggle against sin is very real. So God promises more than just a fresh start. There is forgiveness for yesterday's sins, and also for tomorrow's. Do you think that this will encourage some to feel that they can sin as they like since God will forgive them anyway? It is not so. The people who work hardest to overcome sin are those who feel the debt they owe to the one who has blotted it out. Gratitude is a powerful incentive to live well! James Denney has described gratitude as 'the most intimate, intense and uniform characteristic of New Testament life… It is so profound that the whole being of the Christian is changed by it.'[1]

Chosen, not for good in me,
Wakened up from wrath to flee,
Hidden in the Saviour's side,
By the Spirit sanctified,
Teach me, Lord, on earth to show
By my love how much I owe.

(Robert Murray M'Cheyne, 1813-43)

Have you noticed something? The new covenant is the message of the new birth in Old Testament language. Unless we are born again we cannot see the Kingdom of heaven! It is better than the former covenant because it is all in the hands of God. We can neither earn it nor forfeit if. Think of it: a new nature, a new relationship, a new experience, a new record, and each one a free gift. Jesus says that those who ask receive.

---

1 James Denney, *The Death of Christ*, p.61.

18
A BETTER SANCTUARY

Please read Hebrews 9:1-28

Introduction

The author of this epistle tells us, in great detail, about the priesthood. He invites us to look at Jesus. Compared with him the high priests of Aaron's line no longer have a place in the purposes of God. The author's reason for doing this was to help Jewish converts of the first century. To turn away from their ancestral religion seemed a great sacrifice, but in Jesus they were gaining a greater priest than Aaron or any of his successors. Two thousand years later, the issues are still with us. Only Jesus can reconcile us to God. Both his nature and moral character surpass those of the priests of Israel. Furthermore, God has given him a greater task than theirs. Their ministry was part of an obsolete covenant that would soon vanish away, but Jesus brought in a better covenant founded on better promises. Another area in which Jesus' ministry was greater than theirs concerns the sanctuary. The temple in Jerusalem was one of the glories of the ancient world. It is easy to see why. Even today, in a secular age, some people are greatly attached to the cathedrals that form part of our national heritage. Judaism had but one temple. It dominated the nation's capital, and was the emotional and religious focus for a whole people. Such was its hold on the Jewish imagination that the author of this epistle seemed to ask people to do the impossible – to leave it behind. Though it was so magnificent, the temple belonged to an age when the people of God were in their infancy. Above all, they must not suppose that in giving up the temple they would gain nothing in return. Verse 11 tells us that there is another sanctuary. No stonemason has placed his level against its walls, but it is so grand that the temple in Jerusalem is no more than a *copy and shadow* of it (8:5). The theme before us now is Jesus and his ministry in that *greater and more perfect tabernacle* (11).

The copy and shadow (1–10)

Once again the author invites us to compare. Firstly he shows us the *earthly sanctuary* (1). He wants to show us that it had its limitations. Jesus' disciples once stood outside the temple amazed at its grandeur (Matthew 24:1). How permanent it seemed, but it was part of a system soon to give way to something much better. Verse 10 speaks of *the time of reformation*, when the new order would supersede the old. God never intended the temple and its rituals to last forever. Its role was temporary. During the *present time* (9) it served as a symbol. It bears comparison with the Lord's Supper. The bread and wine are tangible reminders of Jesus and his death for sinners. As such, they are precious to Christian people. Nevertheless, we shall not need them when Jesus returns. They are a means of proclaiming the Lord's death *till he comes* (1 Corinthians 11:26). In the same way, converted Jews could lay aside the temple and all its associated paraphernalia. It had served its purpose. What was that purpose? God had given it as a symbol, a visual aid in stone. It taught a powerful object lesson. The Jewish converts who first read this epistle would have been familiar with the temple built by King Herod the Great[1], but the references in chapter 9 are all to the tabernacle. This is apt, because the tabernacle was erected at the time when the covenant was first made. The temples of later years were stone copies of that tabernacle. Verses 1-5 describe the furnishings, the lamp-stand, table and so on. These things have meaning but the author does not wish us to concentrate upon them. The thing that stands out is that the tabernacle was divided into two distinct sections. There was the *first part* (2), or the *holy place* with its accoutrements, and then, beyond that the *Holiest of All* (3). In between the two sections was a splendid curtain called the *second veil* (the first veil marked the entrance from the court-yard into the first section).

Verse 6 tells us that the *first part*, or *holy place* was in regular use. The priests had to tend the lamp-stand and burn incense every day. Once a week they also had to renew the twelve loaves of the *shewbread*. In contrast, the second veil was pulled aside only on one day every year, the solemn Day of Atone-ment (7). Only the high priest could enter, and only then with the blood of a bull to make atonement for his own sin, and the blood of a goat for the sins of the people. It was a moment of high drama. A sinful man drew near to a holy God. Would God accept his offering? Or would he destroy the sinner for his presumption? (Apparently a rope was placed around his ankle so that he could be hauled out if the encounter with the living God was so overwhelming that he became unconscious and could not make his own way out.) That veil was a potent sym-bol. Its very appearance was forbidding. It was made of blue, gold and scarlet linen and embroidered all over with cherubim, the dread angels who guard the holiness of God. The message was clear: 'Keep out!' In the language of verse 8, the way into the Holy Place was *not yet made manifest*. There was a barrier between God and the people. The real obstacle however, was not the veil. That was merely a vivid symbol. The actual obstacle was sin.

The greater and more perfect tabernacle (11-22)

It is not hard to imagine how the temple in Jerusalem must have appeared. Archaeologists have made replicas. We cannot, however, speculate about the sanctuary where Jesus ministers. It is not made with hands. We must make the leap from the lesser to the greater, from symbol to reality. God is in this perfect tabernacle and Jesus is there as the High Priest of his people. There is something new and thrilling here. When Jesus died, the veil of the temple was torn in two (see Matthew 27:51). Throughout its long history the temple had conveyed the message that God and man were separated. Now something had happened to end the alienation. The heavenly sanctuary has no veil. The way is open. All who belong to Jesus may follow him into the innermost recesses of God's presence and favour. The offerings made all the difference. When the high priests of Israel went behind the curtain once a year, they came out again and it closed behind them once more. Their offerings were not sufficient. Verse 13 mentions atonement, and the purification ritual for those who had touched a dead body. (Anyone who had done that had to be sprinkled with water containing the ashes of a red heifer.) These things were only symbols. As verse 9 says, they left the conscience as it was. An outward ritual can only provide outward cleansing.

Jesus has entered the Most Holy Place with his own blood. This goes to the heart of the problem. The sacrifice of an animal did have a limited value. It could illustrate the principle outlined in verse 22 that *without shedding of blood there is no remission.* Sin demands a price, and that price is blood. Either we, ourselves, pay or someone else must pay for us. Over many centuries the Jewish people had become familiar with the principle that without the shedding of blood there can be no atonement for sin. Ritual bloodshed had been an integral part of their religion. At the same time, however, animal sacrifices had never been truly effective because no bull or calf can take the place of a human being. What can an involuntary, uncomprehending sacrifice do? By contrast, Jesus offered himself to God in the place of his people. He is the ideal substitute; he is just what the sinner needs. We need to be purged (14). We resemble those Israelites who accidentally touched a corpse. The smell of death is upon us. Our best actions are only *dead works* (6:1). They spring from a dead nature. How can the living God have contact with those who are dead inside? The amazing news is that Jesus has offered his spotless life to God in place of our transgressions. Verses 16-17 contain an astonishing idea. Jesus has left us, in his will, his right to be on intimate terms with his Father!

Converted Jews loved the earthly sanctuary. A sense of national heritage bound them to it. Nevertheless, if they had looked below the surface, they would have been glad to finish with it. Its presence, for such a long time, in Jerusalem reminded them that God and man were enemies. Right at the heart of it the veil told the tragic story of a God sealed off from sinners. What a relief to consider the heavenly sanctuary instead! It speaks the glad message of an open door, and a barrier overthrown. Now, all who follow Jesus may join him in his Father's presence. The earthly sanctuary said 'Keep out'; the heavenly sanctuary says 'Come to me ...'

Priestly service that is superior in every way (23-28)

Do you appreciate the greatness of Jesus' High Priesthood? Chapter 9 closes with a comparison between Jesus' ministry in the heavenly sanctuary, and that of the high priest on the day of atonement. On that day he made three appearances. First of all, the high priest would appear before the people at the altar of sacrifice in the temple courtyard. There he would kill the beasts whose blood would be taken into the sanctuary. This corresponds to the incarnation of our Saviour for the purpose of offering up himself. As verse 26 has it, *he has appeared to put away sin by the sacrifice of himself.* There is, however, an important difference. Unlike the high priests of old, Jesus has not had to repeat his offering. Their offerings were never intended to suffice, but to create a longing for something greater. Jesus' offering, however, was enough. God has accepted it. Roman Catholicism teaches that the sacrifice of Christ is re-presented in the Mass. First of all this idea contradicts the teaching of our passage. Secondly it suggests that Jesus' death on the cross was not sufficient to cover all the sin of his people, whereas his sacrifice was offered once and for all (26).

The next appearance of the high priest occurred when he entered the Most Holy Place. This is only a shadow of a far more glorious entry, the Saviour's ascension into heaven. As verse 24 says, he has appeared *in the presence of God.* Furthermore, he has done so *for us.* In some circles the idea of priesthood causes much discussion. Should it be reserved for a privileged élite, or be confined to one sex? We can detach ourselves from all that. First of all we have a better High Priest than all the clergy of Christendom put together. We have Jesus! There is more. A priest is someone who has access into the presence of God. In that case, every follower of Jesus is a priest. Ought women to be priests? Of course! They have been, ever since Jesus appeared before his Father on their behalf. Whether women should be pastors is quite another issue, but I write these words to priests of both sexes.

The high priest's third appearance occurred when he emerged from the sanctuary and the people knew that God had accepted his offering. Jesus will appear once more! This is the message of verse 28. He will come to save. Yes, in one sense we are saved already, but the process of our salvation is not complete. When Jesus comes to this earth *the second time*, every remaining vestige of sin in the believer will be thoroughly purged away. No wonder such people 'wait eagerly'. Oh to be like Jesus! But this is not a hopeless longing. In due course all believers will find that their deepest longings have come true. The Son of God is coming to transform us into his likeness.

Do you 'wait eagerly' for his coming? This idea fills some people with fear. They have reason to fear – verse 27 speaks of judgement, an appointment that all must face. Some people will confront it at Jesus' return, most people at the time of their death. The idea of reincarnation appeals to some. It seems to offer an infinite number of opportunities to be saved. God's Word however, could not be more clear. We have but one life in which to prepare for the next. After death, judgement follows. How crucial that each one of us should ask certain pressing questions. Is Jesus my High Priest? Have I made his sacrifice my own? Can I face God with a clear conscience? Has Jesus opened heaven for me?

---

[1]   This was the third temple to stand on that site. The first was built by King Solomon and the second had been built after the people of Israel returned from exile in Babylon.

19
A BETTER SACRIFICE

Please read Hebrews 10:1-18

Introduction

These verses form the closing part of a major section of this epistle. They conclude the long treatment of a grand subject: the High Priesthood of our Lord Jesus Christ. The aim of the author has been to convince Christian Jews that if they surrendered the faith of their fathers they would gain something so much better in Jesus! Indeed, God intended the religion of the Old Testament to prepare the way for the coming of Christ. On the one hand we have the *law* (1), that is the whole system of religion which Moses gave to Israel at Sinai, and on the other hand we have *the good things to come*, namely the blessings of the new covenant which Jesus brought in. The author has taken us through a series of comparisons. We have been able to compare Jesus with the priests of Aaron's line, the covenants old and new, and the temple of Jerusalem with the heavenly sanctuary where Jesus ministers. Now we make our final comparison. Jesus is greater than the high priests of Israel because he offers a better sacrifice than they did.

Sacrifices that can never take away sins (1-4)

The religion of the Old Testament was defective in one vital area. Its sacrifices could not make those who tried to approach God *perfect* (1). These sacrifices could not make people fit to live in his presence. This deficiency is basic. The whole point of religion is to bring human beings into a relationship with God. Our wayward and sinful lives have alienated us from him, and the breach needs to be mended. Animal sacrifices could never achieve this. The author begins by saying that they were not even intended to do so. Verse 1 explains that they relate to the sacrifice of Jesus as a shadow corresponds to the image that casts it. The shadow does reveal something. It gives us a vague outline, but it is so much better to have the thing itself. Before Jesus came into the world, the offerings on the altar of the temple did teach a valuable lesson, namely that sin offends God and that he demands a sacrifice to appease his wrath (see 9:22). However, these things were only signposts that pointed to a greater offering. Now that Jesus has offered himself to God, his people can leave behind the preparatory system. It has served its purpose and can now fade into the background.

Another flaw in the sacrificial system is that it was repetitive. The author refers to *the same sacrifices ... continually ... year by year* (1). There was no end to it. The pattern was repeated over and over again. This can only mean that the sacrifices were deficient. If it had worked the first time, why go back to the beginning and start again? The fact that the routine went on and on showed that these offerings could not purge a guilty conscience. If, after the Day of Atonement, a worshipper sensed that his sin was completely pardoned, why return the following year and go through the procedure all over again?

Verse 4 is striking. The bulls and goats killed on the Day of Atonement would never suffice as an offering for sin. Human beings had offended God. Terrified animals dragged unwillingly to the altar could never be adequate substitutes for rational beings who deliberately defied their Maker. Those thousands of slaughtered cattle could only be a symbol at best. If an offering were to satisfy God's justice the victim would need to be exactly equivalent to the offender. Man had sinned; man must suffer. Only a voluntary sacrifice could cover the offence.

It is natural to wonder whether there was any point to the old system. What is the good of a system that cannot achieve its purpose? The answer is that it did attain its object. The sacrificial system was never intended to provide a complete remedy for sin. It had a much more limited aim. As verse 3 explains, the sacrifices were a *reminder*. No one must forget that he was guilty before God! The calendar of the Jewish nation included a regular opportunity to confront the fact of personal guilt. Because the Jew had to go to Jerusalem each year with the best of his herd he examined his conscience. This is why the apostle Paul described the law as a *schoolmaster to bring us to Christ* (Galatians 3:24). It was designed from the outset to encourage sorrow for sin, and a desperate longing to be right with God. Those Jews who understood the school-master's lesson understood that this was all part of the spiritual apprenticeship of God's people. The law was training them to look forward, to anticipate something that would match all their expectations, an offering that would indeed take away sins.

The offering that sanctifies (5-10)

When Jesus came into the world (5), the reality that the old system anticipated had now arrived. In making this point the author faced a pastoral problem. He was questioning the traditions that Jewish people loved. In order to reassure them, he appealed to the Old Testament. Thus, verses 5-7 contain a quotation taken from Psalm 40:6–8, which is then explained in verses 8-10. The Jewish Scriptures themselves taught that the sacrifice established in the former covenant would eventually be replaced. Even before the birth of Jesus, Jews accepted that Psalm 40 was a Messianic Psalm, and that the anointed servant of Yahweh was speaking these words. Apparently there was something that pleased the Lord more than sacrificial offerings. This was the willing obedience of his servant. The story of Saul at Gilgal in 1 Samuel 15 teaches the same. King Saul had gained a victory over the Amalekites, but foolishly sacrificed some of the livestock that he had taken, instead of waiting for the arrival of Samuel. In verse 22 Samuel responded to this foolish action by saying,

> Has the Lord as great delight in burnt offerings and sacrifices, as in obeying the voice of the Lord? Behold, to obey is better than sacrifice, and to heed than the fat of rams.

Messiah came to do the will of God. If we are to understand what this meant, a phrase in verse 5 is especially important. The author quotes from Psalm 40:6 and places these words in the mouth of Messiah. He took his quotation from the Greek translation of the Old Testament available at that time, (known as the Septuagint), which gives us the reading: *a body you have prepared for me*. In our Old Testament, which is trans-lated directly from the Hebrew, this reads: 'My ears you have opened.' The word 'opened' can read 'pierced', or 'dug'. This looks back to a ceremony recorded in Exodus 21:1-6. If a Hebrew servant loved his master, and did not want to leave his service after six years, he could ask to stay. He would then have his ear pierced with an awl. This pierced ear was a mark of devotion; it indicated the wish to be a perpetual servant. In that respect, ears represent the whole body. A dutiful servant who listens eagerly for his instructions will obey them with his

whole being. No servant ever loved his Lord better than
Messiah. His obedience was total. Look at Philippians 2:5-8.
The cross was no accident. Nevertheless, how could he obey,
unless a body was prepared for him? The eternal Word could
not die in the place of sinners unless he had a body of flesh and
bone that men could manhandle, beat, scourge and crucify.

The priests of Israel offered the bodies of slaughtered
animals. God's Messiah offered his own body, a sacrifice that
was made in complete contrast to theirs. The bulls and goats
did not know what they faced. Jesus knew, trembled at the
thought of it, but bowed to the will of his Father (See Luke
22:41-44; John 12:27). The beasts before the altar did not
co-operate, but Jesus was a willing victim. Furthermore, it was
human flesh that was torn and broken, human blood that was
spilt. A bull or goat cannot take my place, but a man has done
so. Salvation depends on this. Verse 10 tells us that the will of
God was that his people should be *sanctified* or set apart. In
other words he wanted them to become holy. None but holy
people can enjoy the fellowship of a holy God! If we are to
become holy, something must be done to God! If we are to
become holy, something must be done to remove our guilt.
Jesus has done it! His offering of himself means that he freely
and willingly endured the penalty that we deserve. Verse 9 says
that he has taken away the first *that he may establish the second*. By his death Jesus abolished the bloodstained altar and
all that went with it.

The new is better (11-18)

Verses 11 and 12 leave us in no doubt that Jesus' offering is
superior to the carcasses of dumb animals. Look at the priests
of Israel: they were never off their feet. The temple contained
no chairs whatever, not even a throne for the exalted personage

of the high priest. He had work to do, work that would never cease. No doubt if the temple still stood, the priests of Israel would still be working. How futile! By contrast our priest is seated *at the right hand of God*. This takes us back to chapter 1:13 that quotes Psalm 110. This Psalm clearly predicts that Almighty God would reward Messiah's victory with the place of honour! Why does he sit? In everyday life a working man is able to sit down and relax once he has finished the task in hand. By his death and resurrection, Jesus had accomplished all that was necessary to atone for his people's sins and clear their record with God. Have you ever asked yourself 'What can I do to get right with God?' The answer is, 'Nothing at all, for Jesus accomplished it all years ago.' All that remains is for you to accept Christ's sacrifice as your own.

Look at verse 14. This tells us that *by one offering*, the Lord Jesus *has perfected for ever those who are being sanctified*. The tenses are interesting. Jesus has perfected his people, but they are still being sanctified. There is no conflict. The first statement refers to the Christian's standing before God. If you receive Jesus' sacrifice as an offering to God on your behalf, God credits you with the record of someone who is completely innocent. The second statement reminds us that the actual transformation of our characters is a process that will only be completed when Jesus comes again to make all things new. For now he is waiting until the time comes to subdue all his foes. As we grapple with our sins, we sometimes wonder why he waits. Would it not be better if he brought everything to a head right now? He waits for the sake of those yet to believe. Think of it: the Lord has already delayed his return almost 2,000 years so that you could make your peace with him! Are we not torn here? We long for his coming, and the end of our debilitating struggle against sin, but we also want him to wait a little while, just long enough for our children to be converted.

These are thrilling verses. One act has purchased a pardon that lasts forever. It has dealt with all our sin. I pity those poor souls who believe in the Mass. They are back in a world of shadows; they need to repeat a sacrifice again and again. Sunday may be a 'state of grace' but on Monday you need a fresh sacramental pardon. Jesus offers something far better: a pardon that is complete in every way, total remission of sins. Verse 16 reminds us of a promise from Jeremiah 31 concerning God's new covenant. God will not remember his people's sins. He chooses to treat us as though we had never committed those lawless deeds. Do we appreciate what Jesus has accomplished? His offering has written off the guilty past of every believer, and made him or her new people. What a High Priest!

20
'LET US DRAW NEAR'

Please read Hebrews 10: 19-39

Introduction

These verses introduce us to the closing section of the epistle. The emphasis is practical. We are to build on what we have learned in the earlier sections. Verses 19 to 21 form a bridge between the preceding and the following verses. In the first place, believers can approach God with *boldness* (19). There need be no fear or uncertainty. God will accept them because he has accepted the blood offering of Jesus, their priest. The second statement in verse 20 builds on this. The way to God that Jesus has opened is *new*. Not only has it replaced the old way, but it will never be superseded. In the days of the former covenant, ordinary worshippers could not enter the most holy place in the temple. The veil blocked their path. Everything changed when it was torn in two. That is why Jesus' body is compared to the veil. God is only accessible to sinners because Jesus' flesh was torn. Verse 21 sums up the middle part of the whole epistle. We have a High Priest! We need not be anxious about life in God's presence. Someone who loves us is there to smooth the path. These things are to affect the way we live. Because they are true, certain practical consequences follow. Note the sequence of thought in verses 19-22: *Therefore ... having boldness ... let us draw near.*

Let us draw near (22-25)

Here is a warm-hearted invitation to live in the presence of God. The word *us* (22) is important. The author includes himself along with his readers. Why be hesitant? Why stay at a distance? Everything has been done to make it possible for us to live in the closest contact with God. Jesus has died for his people. Let us together take advantage of this. The Almighty invited us to a life of friendship with him. We need not be shy. Love is beckoning. Jesus has done his work.

Jesus has not only done something for his people, he has done something in them. Where is a *true heart* (22) to come from? The Bible tells us in Jeremiah 17:9 that the human heart is deceitful and desperately wicked. Furthermore, we are inconsistent and fickle. Something must change a person if he is to draw near to God with *full assurance of faith*. What has happened to produce steadiness in the place of vacillation? Verse 22 takes us back to the ceremony of the temple, and reminds us that the priests did not merely offer sacrifices. They also had to wash themselves. An enormous vessel called the laver was placed close to the altar for this very purpose. This outward washing of the body was a symbol. In that respect it has similarities to Christian baptism. Water may cleanse the body, but we also need to have our consciences cleansed (1 Peter 3:21). There is only one way to free the conscience from guilt, and that is to assure it that someone else has taken that guilt upon himself.

This offers further encouragement to us to draw near to God. If we are no longer guilty in his sight, he has no cause to turn us away. Indeed, he intends us to draw near and then stay. Verse 23 stresses that we must *hold fast* and not waver. Our relationship with God is not meant to be tentative. Jesus did not die for his own people and give them clean hearts so that they could then follow him inconsistently. Other believers are enormously important here. Let us *consider one another*, says verse 24. We all have moments of instability and weakness. How good it is to have others who have spurred us on! Encouragement can be a potent force. The highlight of the Soccer season in England is the FA (Football Association) Cup. I remember the FA Cup campaign of 1973 because three times that year, Sunderland, my home town club, did the impossible. Then a second division side, they took on first division opponents and won, including the mighty Arsenal and the favourites, Leeds United. The Town was silent on match days, but the stadium at Roker Park wasn't. 50,000 people gave tongue to the hopes of half a county. Now think of a church where the pastor is declaring the unsearchable riches of Christ with clarity and fervour. Each time he makes a fresh statement about the greatness of the gospel, the congregation rises as one man to urge him on. If it seems a bit far-fetched, the traffic is not one-way. If preaching can affect a congregation, a congregation can also affect the preaching.

Who is responsible to stir Christians up to *love and good works* (24)? In many churches the answer is that it is the task of the pastor, and perhaps the elders. By contrast it is clear from verses 24 and 25 that everyone's perseverance is the responsibility of everyone else. Competitors in a contest spur each other on. Encouragement in the biblical sense is often something hearty and vigorous. In the city of Bayeux in Northern France, there is a famous tapestry commemorating the conquest of England by the Normans in 1066. In one section of this tapestry, Bishop Odo, the half brother of William the Conqueror, is shown rounding up a number of nervous knights who wanted to quit the fight. He encouraged them with a club! The Latin reads 'Odo confortat pueros,' or 'Odo strengthens the lads.' Do we make an active effort to put heart into one another?

The writer emphasises, one *good work* in particular. We are to stir each other up into assembling together (25). This is more than casual contact between believers (it stems from a word meaning assembling in the synagogue). We are not to forsake the meetings of our own local churches. Why is this so important? It will help us to *hold fast* (23). It is a matter of simple observation that those who do not come together consistently for the apostles' doctrine, breaking of bread, fellowship and prayer (Acts 2:42), tend to be those who are most likely to waver. When we are at a low ebb ourselves, we appreciate encouragement. We all benefit from it, so let us create a climate where this kind of encouragement becomes infectious. It does matter! The *Day* is approaching. Life is too short to be wasted. Only three things really count: *faith* (22), *hope* (23), and *love* (24). When the Son of Man comes, will he find faith on earth?

The danger of failing to draw near (26-31)

Verse 26 issues a solemn warning. It speaks of a sin so wilful that no sacrifice can atone for it. This takes us back to the Law of Moses. The system of sacrifices distinguished between sins committed in ignorance, and those committed *with a high hand* (Numbers 15:27-31). The sin mentioned in this verse, is something even more heinous than such defiant breaches of the Law of Moses. It is the sin of apostasy. Verse 29 describes it with three graphic expressions. Firstly, rejecting Jesus and all he stands for amounts to treading him *underfoot*. Far from respecting the Son of God, such a person tramples on him as a victorious soldier might trample on the carcass of a despised enemy. Secondly, falling away from a profession of faith amounts to treating the *blood of the covenant* as though it were a common thing. Picture a person who once claimed that Jesus had made him clean. Now he regards that blood as having no special meaning at all. This person has rejected the work of Jesus, deciding in effect that all his suffering is nothing. Thirdly, his departure from the gospel is also an insult to the Holy Spirit. In grace and mercy the Spirit of God has brought a measure of enlightenment, only to be shunned. What kind of person has committed such a vile sin? Those first century Jews who professed faith in Christ had taken a stand for the new covenant; they would sooner have Jesus than the old system of sacrifices. Suppose that some of them, under threat of persecution, later reverted to Judaism. Were they not saying that the old was as good as the new, and that Jesus may as well not have died?

Apostasy is still a real danger. It happens when we put our hands to the plough only to look back (Luke 9:62). It happens to those who draw near, but then fall away. It is the condition of the people who start by saying that they will rely on Jesus for salvation, and nothing else, only to say some time later that they expect to be in heaven as a reward for their merits. Their position could not be more serious. Two *fearful* things await them. The first is God's judgement (27), the other is God himself (31). Some people are shocked by this idea. How could falling into the hands of God be dreadful? Could the God who is love be terrifying? Indeed he does love! He loves his gracious Son, and the tender Spirit, but those who arrogantly turn their backs on both play a dangerous game. They touch the very apple of his eye. Jesus' parable of the wicked vine-dressers in Mark 12:1–12 is most instructive. After many provocations, the Lord of the vineyard sent his son. *They will respect my Son*, he said, but in fact the vine-dressers killed him. Jesus followed with a question that needs no answer. *What will the owner of the vineyard do?* What became of Judas? Here is a powerful incentive for staying close to God all our days. We must never give Satan, the world, or our own hearts the least reason to think that we might prove to be apostates at the last. Who could reject Jesus, the gentle shepherd of the sheep? Even now, people trample him underfoot. Do not be one of them!

Drawing strength from the past (32–39)

How would the Hebrew believers respond to this challenge? Would there be a closer walk with God, or would they prove by falling away, that all along they were no more true disciples than Judas had been? We can see from verse 39 that the author thought well of them. In these closing verses he tried to spur them on by reminding them of how their Christian lives began. Those had been good days. Soon after they were *enlightened* (32) they had faced a number of stern challenges, and emerged with faith intact. They had suffered persecution themselves, having become a conspicuous target for the malice of others. In addition, they willingly sought out other victims of tribulation, and stood by them, knowing that this made them all the more vulnerable (33). The author himself had benefited from their kindness (34). They had shown real quality, having reached the state of mind where they could see their property and goods destroyed without being embittered by their loss. They could calmly say goodbye to their belongings, knowing that something of much greater value awaited them.

The author addressed these words to the believers who had become wobbly, fearful weaklings. The challenge is straightforward: 'You have not always been like this! You can persevere, you have done it before. Live up to the standards that you set for yourselves!' Their good start was much more significant than their subsequent backsliding. He challenged them to regain that earlier intense devotion. Like the church at Ephesus, they had lost their *first love* (Revelation 2:4) and must recapture the ardour of yesterday! Perhaps he also speaks to us at this point. How sad if the Christian that we used to be shames the Christian that we have become. *Recall the former days* (32).

The mark of the true disciple is endurance. Verse 38 includes a well-known quotation from Habakkuk 2:3-4, *the just shall live by faith*. This does not refer to a person who believed 'once upon a time'. It speaks of a life where faith is an abiding and continuing reality. Does this talk of endurance sound bleak? No doubt some are tempted to stray because the tribulation never seems to end; there is no relief, it just goes on and on. But it will not last forever. Faith in Jesus is faith in someone who is coming. A little earlier we noted that the time is short. This is a spur to endeavour. *The night is coming when no one can work* (John 9:4). At the same time, it is a comforting thought. Life will not always be blood and toil, tears and sweat. We are like the garrison of Lucknow in the Indian Mutiny, completely surrounded, with the situation seemingly hopeless. But wait: an old Scots lady can just hear the faint note of bagpipes. That wild music tells its own story. Relief is on its way! General Havelock is coming, with a regiment of Highlanders. All that the garrison has to do is to hold on. Our general too is on his way. In the meantime, he has left us this instruction: *Do business till I come* (Luke 19:13).

21

LESSONS IN FAITH FROM THE DAWN OF TIME

Please read Hebrews 11:1-7

Introduction (1-2)

The Hebrew Christians who first received this letter needed one thing above all others: faith. We are the same. Like them, we claim to believe in Christ, and we also face things that test our claim. Do we go on? Do we make progress? It would be wrong to think that we need faith at the beginning of the Christian life, but have no need for it afterwards. The life of a disciple not only begins with faith; it is a life of faith. The journey commences when we place our trust in Jesus for the first time. We make progress as we continue to place our trust in him. The whole purpose of Chapter 11 is to encourage Christians to go on in faith.

In verse 1 the author gives a description of the kind of faith that he longed to see in his readers. First of all, it is *the substance of things hoped for*. In the author's mind, *faith* is linked with *hope*. It looks forward to the future with serene confidence. It is based on the conviction that God is reliable, therefore we can be assured that he will be gracious in the future. We have not yet experienced the fulfilment of God's promises, any more than the heroes of the Old Testament era had done when their earthly lives ended, but what we know of God leaves us in no doubt that our hope will *not disappoint us*

(Romans 5:5). There is a marked contrast here between hope as the Christian experiences it and hope as it is understood in everyday life. When most people talk about their hopes the element of confidence is entirely absent. They have certain longings and aspirations but the future is random and unpredictable. The outcome is by no means guaranteed. The author, however, links hope with faith so that his readers can dispel any element of uncertainty from their minds. Given that we can be confident in God now, we can equally confident of his intentions toward us in the future. We can *hold fast the confession of our hope without wavering, for He who promised is faithful* (10:23).

The word rendered *substance*[1] in our version translates a Greek word with a range of possible meanings. The same word is used in 1:3 to describe the being or the *person* of God. It therefore suggests that faith makes our hopes substantial. It takes hold of the things that God has promised, even though those things have not yet come about, and makes them real in our experience. The original term can also mean 'foundation'. Faith lays the foundation on which the building of our hopes is erected. In 3:14 the same word is actually translated *confidence*. (We are encouraged to *hold the beginning of our confidence steadfast to the end.*) Faith, then, gives us the assurance that the things we hope for will indeed come to pass. In the secular Greek of the first century, the same word could also mean 'guarantee'. Understood in that way, faith takes possession of our future blessings. It makes our enjoyment of them certain and in doing so, gives us a foretaste of them in the here and now. Taken together, these different shades of meaning all reinforce the author's message. Faith looking into a future that appears fraught with uncertainties is unshakeable, knowing that God will stand by his promises.

The author goes on to describe faith as *the evidence of things not seen*. It involves placing our trust in things that we cannot see, but which are real nevertheless. For instance, Christians believe in heaven. They expect to go there when they die, and are certain that Jesus is there now, praying for them. Does this mean that believers are gullible people, ready to commit themselves to something that they cannot prove? No, faith is not a gamble. It is based on knowledge. Look at verse 6. God himself cannot be seen. He cannot be detected by our physical senses. Nevertheless, the man of faith recognises not only that God exists but also that the person who seeks him will be amply repaid. Verse 2 tells us that we are not the first people to have faced the challenge of walking by faith and not by sight. We have spiritual ancestors, the *elders*. God's servants of long ago are an example to us.

Case Study One: Faith and the Creation (3)

Verse 3 takes us right back to the beginning of all things. The origin of the universe mystifies people. Many do not accept the verdict of Scripture. Nevertheless, some argue that this debate is between those with faith on the one hand, and those who rely on scientific observation on the other. Honesty compels us to admit that, in the area of origins, no one can claim first-hand knowledge. The Almighty asked the patriarch Job a question: *Where were you when I laid the foundations of the earth?* (Job 38:4). No observer was present to record the awesome events of creation. All that can be done is to attempt to reason back from the world that we now have, seeking to make deductions about the way it all began. The alternative, of course, is to accept that God has revealed the truth in his Word. Whatever your view of origins, you exercise faith. Either you trust what God has said, or you have faith in the conclusions of whatever school of scientific thought most appeals to you.

This verse invites us to consider the world that we can see, the natural order that we can observe and measure. We are told that it was *not made of things which are visible*. God did

not take something, which was already there, only to rearrange
it into its present form. The doctrine of creation tells us that
once there was nothing at all but God himself. Then he
created; he brought into being things other than himself. We
are not so much being asked to put our faith in creation, but in
the God who creates. If God merely took a universe that
already existed, and then modified it, this raises all sorts of
questions. Is there someone else in the picture? Some mysterious
being, further back than the God of the Bible? This matters
very much. If forces, other than God, control him, then however great he might be, he is not altogether God. Because he
called the universe into being at the beginning he is Almighty.
He is dependent on no one, and answerable to no one. Faith
looks to a God who is the Lord of beginnings, of endings and
middles. The entire process is under his direction and his alone.
Those who do not bow to the Creator have dethroned God in
their minds. The author of this epistle calls his readers to have
faith. This is not a call to suspend their rational faculties, but to
recognise how great God is.

Case Study Two: Faith and Redemption (4)

This chapter is a portrait gallery in prose. It contains the stories
of many heroes from Old Testament days. The writer is not
simply describing faith in the abstract; he is encouraging ordinary people to live by faith. We grasp principles more easily
when we see them acted out by people with whom we can
identify. There is great value in having role models. If you look
at the people whose stories are recorded here you see faith in
action. The first is Abel, the son of Adam and Eve. What was
the difference between Abel and his brother Cain? We must not
think that Abel was so good that he earned God's blessing. No
human being is capable of doing all that God requires! This
story, recorded for us in the early verses of Genesis 4, is the

story of two sinners, both of whom felt the need to get right with God. That is a question that concerns everyone on earth. Since God is angry with us because of our sin, what can be done to appease his wrath?

The two men produced different answers. Cain cultivated the soil, and brought an offering of agricultural produce. Abel sacrificed the first animals of his flock. Perhaps he remembered that God provided Adam and Eve with clothing made from two slaughtered animals (Genesis 3:21). At any rate, the choice is significant. Abel, it seems, understood the principle of Hebrews 9:22, *without shedding of blood there is no remission*. He knew he could hope for his guilt to be transferred to a substitute. There is more that we need to understand. In later years offerings of foodstuffs were an acceptable part of the sacrificial system, yet the prophets often condemned the people's burnt offerings. It wasn't just enough to get the details of the ritual right. God accepted Abel's offering because the attitude of his heart was correct (Genesis 4:4). Cain saw his offering as a way of insuring himself against possible risks. Abel, on the other hand, saw that he could not appease God with a special gift, as though the Almighty could be humoured. He knew what God was like, and glimpsed something of what he requires if sin is to be covered. Nor did his faith stop there. Knowing these things to be true, he acted upon them. Faith is more than a matter of holding correct opinions. If our convictions do not drive us to action they are not worth much. Many a person has been intellectually convinced that the only way to experience peace with God is to have faith in Christ, without ever actually coming to Christ for pardon. It is not enough to admire Jesus. We must follow him.

Case Study Three: Faith and Final Salvation (5-6)

We come now to the case of Enoch. We do not know much

about this man. We have a short statement in the book of Genesis (5:21-24), quoted in part in verse 5. Sometimes a few words can say a great deal! Enoch's faith affected more than his opinions. It had an effect on his whole life. He *walked with God*. Imagine someone going through life as though God were always with him, as though he and God went through life side by side, with the close familiarity of old and trusted friends. If we were convinced, as Enoch was, that the Almighty was our close companion, would we continue to read certain things, go to such and such places, talk about certain subjects? Would it make a difference to our everyday behaviour if we were conscious that Jesus was there with us?

Why did God take Enoch to himself? He did so for the same reason that he takes any of his people. He loves them, their friendship, and their company. Look at John 17:4. Jesus wants to have his friends with him. If we are Christians, the destiny of Enoch will be yours and mine too. In his case, physical death did not intervene. Those believers who are alive and remain at the time of our Lord's return will experience something similar; they will be caught up to meet him in the air. The end result is the same for all God's people, for the *dead in Christ will rise first* (1 Thessalonians 4:16-17). The Christian's story has a happy ending. It has not happened yet, and therefore it belongs to the realm of things we cannot see. Nevertheless, faith is confident of the outcome because it is confident in the God who has promised. Enoch reminds us that true faith is active. In his case, it was not confined to his opinions; it shaped the man that he became.

The author highlights the particular case of Enoch because it illustrates the general principle in verse 6, *without faith it is impossible to please him*. Live without faith in God and we say, in effect, that our own resources are sufficient, that we have no need of the Almighty. As Philip Hughes has said, 'The man without faith is the man who wickedly attempts to suppress the truth about God (Romans 1:18ff.). He cannot possibly be included in the number of those who please God. To repudiate faith is to sever the lifeline which links the creature to his creator and is thus to lose the very meaning and purpose of one's existence. It is to be without God and therefore without hope in the world.' (Ephesians 2:12)[2] By contrast, faith operates on the assumption that God *is*, that he truly exists. Seeking God is not a matter of chasing shadows. Instead, it is the confident search for one who will reward those who come seeking him. (We ought to note in passing that the author does not mean to suggest that God rewards our good deeds but rather that he is rewarding all that his grace has brought about in our lives.)

Case Study Four: Faith and the Judgement to come (7)

The patriarch Noah is an excellent example of faith at work in a human life. Faith sets a man apart from his contemporaries. Noah knew something that the other people of his day would not acknowledge. God warned him that he was going to destroy the world by water. This drove him to action. First of all, he became a preacher of righteousness (see 2 Peter 2: 5). He had the painful duty of condemning the world. This does not mean that he took a perverse delight in savage denunciations for their own sake. He was concerned for people. He knew that they had been lulled into a false sense of security. In the second place, *he prepared an ark for the saving of his household*. Imagine the ridicule that would have come his way. We do not know whether he lived anywhere near the sea, and it seems likely that the world before the flood had no rain. How absurd! Yet Noah's faith sustained his preaching and his building for 120 years. The unseen world was more real to him than the false understanding of his short-sighted neighbours. Noah knew that *it is a fearful thing to fall into the hands of the living God* (10:31).

Do we have the same kind of faith that Noah had? We know the outcome of all things. We worship the God of endings, and he has revealed that a terrible fate awaits those who will not make their peace with him.

It is a righteous thing with God to repay with tribulation those who trouble you, and to give you who are troubled rest with us when the Lord Jesus is revealed from heaven with His mighty angels, in flaming fire taking vengeance on those who do not know God, and on those who do not obey the gospel of our Lord Jesus Christ. These will be punished with everlasting destruction from the presence of the Lord and from the glory of His power, when he comes, in that day, to be glorified in his saints and to be admired among all those who believe (2 Thessalonians 1:7-10).

Perhaps you are not a Christian. Can you read words like this without longing to get right with God? Like Noah, believers know the only way of escape. Does this affect the way that we pray? Are we sometimes inhibited by the knowledge that if we are as faithful as Noah was, the world will be as hostile to us as it was to him? Is there something that we can do to overcome our fear of the world? The heroes of the faith saw the unseen realities and were held by them. We need God's message to take such a hold on us that other considerations cease to matter. The apostle Paul knew what this meant. Look at 2 Corinthians 5:11, 14. Are we so conscious of what the terror of the Lord will mean to men that we are seized with an urgent desire to persuade them? Does the love of Christ grip us with such intensity that the only thing we can do is proclaim it? If faith does not make a difference, it is not faith.

---

[1]   The Greek word is hypostasis.
[2]   Philip Edgecumbe Hughes, *A Commentary on the Epistle to the Hebrews*, p.460.

22
LESSONS IN FAITH FROM THE LIFE OF ABRAHAM

Please read Hebrews 11:8-16

Introduction

Above all else, Christians need faith. This was true of the
Jewish believers who first received this letter, and it is just as
true of us. What is faith like? One of the best ways to understand faith is to watch it in action. (We learn many things in life
by watching others.) With this in mind, the author introduces
us to the patriarch Abraham. We are invited to consider him as
a case-study in faith. We can see how his faith moulded his
behaviour. Abraham met many challenges and obstacles
during his long life. He learned to respond to them in faith. By
observing him closely, we can learn to do the same.

Starting out in faith (8)

Some people seem to think that faith is just a matter of accepting that certain views about God and his gospel are true. Was
Jesus truly born of a virgin? Did he really rise from the tomb on
the third day? There is no doubt that these things are very
important. We cannot afford to be mistaken in these areas.
Nevertheless, faith involves much more than our opinions. A
person with genuine faith will not merely hold certain convictions,

he will be willing to base his whole life upon them. Faith is an active response to the call of God. God called Abraham to leave the land of his fathers. He obeyed that call. In the same way, a Christian is not simply a person who believes that the Bible is true. He is someone who knows that Jesus has summoned him to leave his old way of life behind. He has responded to the challenge to deny himself, take up his cross, and follow Jesus.

Such faith makes demands. People who knew Abraham when he lived in Ur of the Chaldees must have been astonished to see him set out on a journey that seemed to lead nowhere. Abraham himself did not know *where he was going* (8). Archaeologists tell us that Ur then was the cradle of civilisation. Abraham lived there when it was at the peak of its greatness. It was situated in fertile Mesopotamia. It was the greatest centre of commerce and culture the world had yet seen, a place of bustle and vitality, and Abraham left all that for an uncertain future with no prospects. Where would it all end? No doubt there were people who tried to dissuade him. How many of us, on the point of surrender to Christ, have imagined, or maybe even heard the voices of friends or loved ones begging us not to go through with it: 'Think what you're giving up!' Many people hear the call of God; those with faith respond to it.

The person with faith sees what others cannot see. Abraham had reached the conclusion that a settled life of comfort in Mesopotamia wasn't worth keeping in comparison to a life spent serving God. He knew what really mattered. He was like the man in Jesus' story about the 'pearl of great price' (see Matthew 13:45-46). He saw something so wonderful that nothing else mattered. Never mind the values and preferences of others, something had transformed his whole outlook. Christians are in the same position. Jesus means so much that everything else is worthless in comparison. Do you see life from this perspective? Could you say goodbye to the world and all that it offers as long as you have the friendship of Jesus? Abraham had no idea where he was going, but he knew who was going with him, and that made all the difference.

Going on in faith (9-10)

Christians never get beyond the need for faith. The Christian life begins when we first trust Christ. It continues as our trust deepens and matures. This was the case with Abraham. The adventure of faith was not over when he arrived in Palestine. In one sense, he had reached his journey's end, but conditions were far from settled. *By faith, he sojourned in the land of promise as in a foreign country* (9). The man who had once lived in the greatest city of that age had become a Bedouin, a nomad. We read in Genesis 12:8 that he *built* an altar, but *pitched* his tent. This tells us a great deal about his priorities. He provided for his spiritual needs in a much more permanent and enduring way than he provided for his material needs. The martyr Stephen said that Abraham did not own enough of Canaan to set his foot on (Acts 7:5). Indeed he only purchased some ground when he needed a burial plot for his wife Sarah. He lived the whole of his life in Canaan like a stranger who had no roots, and might suddenly leave it. Five hundred years were to pass before that land became a permanent home for Abraham's descendants. How like the Christian! Do we move through this world like strangers who do not really belong? It is not our natural environment. It would be wise not to become too emotionally attached to it. After all, we are only passing through.

The life of faith can be hard work. That is because Christians are not like other people. The people around us throw all their energies into this world. It is all that they have. Believers however, travel with the minimum of luggage. Meanwhile we have to live with the fact that the people all around us cannot understand our motives. They think that we are strange. At times they are even hostile. What keeps the person with faith going? Abraham kept going because he knew what lay ahead. What can the city of Ur offer to the man who marches with confident pace towards the city of God? Abraham had his vision fixed on something even more delightful than the most glorious of ancient cities, *the city which has foundations, whose builder and maker is God* (10). Better things lay ahead. He could not be sure of the details, but the goal was entrancing. God had a place for him, an everlasting and secure place. What about you? Where is home? A village, town or city somewhere on the surface of this planet? I hope not! God has a new heaven and a new earth waiting for his own people. This world is just the barren wilderness that we pass through on our way to it.

Faith's reward (11-12)

Verse 1 refers to the birth of Isaac. This itself was a triumph of faith. In the first instance, it was the faith of Abraham himself. God had made a covenant with him, which promised that he would become the father of a great people. Secondly, this passage also draws attention to the faith of Sarah his wife. At first sight this might seem strange to those who know the story recorded in Genesis 18. When the Lord appeared to Abraham and promised him that a son would be born in a year's time Sarah laughed. Where is the faith in that? Perhaps she thought that God was mocking her. She was past the age of childbearing. (The problem did not lie with Abraham. He was still capable of fathering children. His son Ishmael was born to his wife's maid Hagar). Many of us have laughed with Sarah. The thing that we most want is withheld from us, so bitterness overwhelms us. Bitterness is so destructive. It easily spreads to others. How often have we felt our enthusiasm and faith to be dampened by the sourness of another?

Sarah's story does not end there. Although it began with her hysterical, unbelieving laughter it ended in faith. This is because the Lord was good to her. He did not explode in wrath and say, 'How dare you!' Look at Genesis 18:13-14.

> The LORD said to Abraham, 'Why did Sarah laugh, saying, "Shall I surely bear a child, since I am old?" Is anything too hard for the LORD? At the appointed time I will return to you, according to the time of life, and Sarah shall have a son.'

Observe the note of reassurance: think again Sarah! *Is anything too hard for the LORD?* And Sarah believed. Our God is very tender. Our faith is very weak at times, but he does not despise it. He is so gentle that he will not break a bruised reed or quench smoking flax (see Isaiah 42:1-4). He nurses the faith of his fearful people as a gardener takes care over a delicate and fragile plant. Faith is not rewarded because we have great amounts of it. Faith only makes a difference when it is faith in a God of infinite love and boundless power.

The reward was out of all proportion to Abraham's faith. That one man has become the father of an incalculable multitude. The author has more in mind here than merely the Jewish race. Abraham has other children! (See Romans 4:16-17). God's promise to the patriarch has reverberated down the centuries. God is still rewarding Abraham's faith. Every time a person comes to living faith in Christ, the number of Abraham's children is increased. Think of all the stars in the galaxies, and all the grains of sand at the edge of the vast oceans. Those who share Abraham's faith are as countless as that. We Christians are not an insignificant clique! This is not because faith is great, but because it rests in the promises and character of a great God. Look at Ephesians 3:20-21. God's ability to perform great things is not limited by our ability to ask! He is able to give more than any earthly king can give. Abraham and Sarah only saw the beginnings of this. Isaac and Jacob were born before Abraham died, but his faith continues to have its effect down to this age and perhaps beyond. Don't despair of praying because you do not see all the answers immediately. Your children may yet be astonished at the fruit of your faith.

Persistent faith (13-16)

When faith is allowed to grow and mature, when it becomes habitual, it perseveres. Verse 13 tells us that Abraham, Isaac and Jacob not only lived in faith, they *died* in it. The approach of death did not shatter their confidence in God. Even though the promises had not yet been fulfilled, the patriarchs left this world serene and calm knowing that God had his own time, and that all would be very well. Each one went to his grave at the end of a long life without having received the promises. Not one of them felt that God had cheated or betrayed them. They knew that God was not playing with them. Having seen the promises in the distance, they were assured of the outcome and hugged those promises tightly to themselves.

It would have been so easy to give it all up, and return to the country that they had left behind. Familiar things exert a powerful pull. We have often seen people emigrate to another country only to return a year or two later. The Hebrew Christians who received this letter faced this temptation in a very acute form. They had set out to follow Jesus, and who could tell how it would all end? What would become of them? The old life seemed so attractive at such times. They were like the Israelites in the wilderness pining for the leeks and garlic of Egypt. We too sense the pull of the old life. Old friendships and old habits often lure us back in the most seductive way. What should we do when we are faced with this kind of temptation?

Go on, or go back? Faith persists, because when the crisis is upon us it knows where our real *homeland* (14) is. The country that we have left is not home, and the country we inhabit now is not home either. The better *country* that we seek lies ahead (16). Some of us are almost there, treading on the very border of Emmanuel's country. With this prospect before us, let us learn faith's lesson. When the siren songs of the old life encourage us to slip back, let us go on. Lost ground is not easily recovered.

Does the struggle seem hard at times? Verse 16 tells us that God knows. He sees his people as they wrestle on towards heaven, and he is *not ashamed* of them! This means that he takes pride in them. He is thrilled with them. This truth is too wonderful for words. It is our privilege and delight to take our name from Jesus. It is a grand thing to claim the title Christian! It means that we belong to Jesus! Sometimes, to our sorrow, we are ashamed of him. Now consider this: how does God wish to be known throughout eternity? He is not ashamed to be the God of Abraham, Isaac, Jacob, Spurgeon, Lloyd-Jones, and countless struggling saints. His joy is to be associated with their small victories and triumphs. He considers it no disgrace to be known as their God. Is this God yours? Who could have a better friend?

23
LESSONS IN FAITH FROM THE PATRIARCHS

Please read Hebrews 11:17-22

Introduction

I once heard about a young man who applied for a post in a further education college. He seemed well qualified. He claimed a number of examination successes, including one in Irish. He could not have known that his interviewer had grown up speaking Scots Gaelic, which is so close to Irish that people speaking either language can often understand one another. After a sentence or two, the young man was found out. He thought his claim would not be tested. And while he lost the chance of a job, he learned a valuable lesson in return. In the same way, if we say that we have faith in God, that claim will be tested. The Apostle Peter tells us that genuine faith is more precious than gold (1 Pet 1:7). Sooner or later, God will try it. The Jewish Christians who first read this letter knew all about that. Persecution and hardship had placed a severe strain on their willingness to trust God. Christians in every age experience the same trial. That is why the author points us to the Patriarchs of Israel. Each one had living faith, but in different ways each faced a stiff challenge. The first readers of the Epistle were not the only people whose faith has faced difficulties, and neither are we.

Faith when the will of God seems impossible (17-19)

Here we have another lesson in faith from the life of Abraham. It is taken from the incident recorded in Genesis 22, where God tested Abraham by requiring him to sacrifice his son Isaac. That word 'test' is extremely important. God was not trying to find out whether Abraham had faith or not: he already knew that. The test was for Abraham's benefit. When it was over, he knew that his faith was real, and more importantly, that he had placed his trust in the right person. In a sense, God put himself on trial. The patriarch's dilemma was acute. God appeared to require two contradictory things. On the one hand he had promised to make Abraham's descendants a great nation, and linked this specifically to Isaac (Genesis 21:12), who as yet was unmarried and without children. On the other hand, God seemed to want the boy dead. What are we to do when God seems to contradict himself? Many believers today are troubled because God holds all men responsible for their eternal destiny, while insisting that the salvation of those who believe is all of his grace. Am I saved because of my decision, or his? Sadly, some conclude that both cannot be right at the same time, and choose which they prefer.

Abraham was torn in two trying to puzzle out the ways of God. Furthermore, the fact that his own son was involved made the trial all the more difficult to bear. God was not simply asking Abraham to consent to Isaac's death: he wanted him to kill Isaac with his own hands, and then live out his days with a distraught Sarah. We too may face moments when obedience to God threatens to bring disaster upon us. The first century Hebrew believers had been rejected by their fellow Jews. Some of us may have met agonising situations where faithfulness to God only seems to cause our worst nightmares. Abraham faced both a personal tragedy, and the terrible possibility that the God who had befriended him was actually a monster who played with his servants as a cat plays with a mouse.

How does faith respond at such times? Abraham reasoned with himself on the basis of what he already knew of God. He concluded that the Almighty would never go back on a promise. If Isaac had to die, God would raise him to life again. This explains Abraham's confidence in Genesis 22:5 when he said to his servants *we will come back to you*. In a real sense, he got his son back from the dead, for although he did not actually kill him, within his heart he had already sacrificed Isaac. Not only did his faith stand the test, but also he now knew as never before that God was worthy of his trust. What of ourselves? Do we have faith? Without it *it is impossible to please him* (6). What kind of faith is it? Will it stand the test? Many have faith when they are healthy only to find that it evaporates when they are sick. When the trial comes, let us profit from Abraham's example. How has God dealt with us in the past? Have we any reason to suppose that he will desert us when we are in difficulties?

Faith tested by mediocrity (20)

Next we are told about the faith of Isaac himself. Verse 20 speaks of the occasion recorded in Genesis 27 when, as an old man, he gave his blessing to his sons, Jacob and Esau. This was an act of faith. When the old man spoke his words of blessing, he passed on a revelation from God concerning their future, and indeed that of their descendants. As soon as he realised that he had been tricked into giving the blessing of the firstborn to Jacob, who was the younger, he refused to revoke it. It was a word from the Almighty, and though his natural preference would have been to see Esau preferred over Jacob, he bowed to the will of God.

Humanly speaking, the situation was unfortunate. Isaac seemed unable to escape the limitations of his background. Younger sons did not receive the inheritance of their older brothers! God however, is not bound by the ties of culture, and convention. Rebekah for her part operated from a mixture of motives. Genesis 25:23 records that she was given a prophecy just prior to the birth of her sons, that the older would serve the younger! She was not above helping God's plan forward with stratagems of her own. She devised a comprehensive plan whereby Jacob deceived his father. All Isaac's senses failed him in the face of Jacob's trickery. The broth he tasted, the voice he heard, and the person he touched were not what he supposed them to be. In the meantime, Jacob learned that nothing is impossible for an unscrupulous fellow with a fertile imagination. He did not learn better until several decades had passed. Each character in the story is familiar to us, for the Church of today is full of people like them. They are real people with the usual mixture of spiritual strengths and weaknesses. We cannot always identify with spiritual superheroes; they are so remote from us, but Isaac is a type that we recognise. Spiritual gold was mixed with a great deal that was impure, but God regarded it. As we look at ourselves in the tangled web of daily life, much will discourage us. What a bundle of contradictions and compromises we can be! Nevertheless, if real faith is present, however small, God will not despise it.

Faith tested by hard knocks (21)

Jacob is our next case-study. We meet him, as we met Isaac, towards the end of life, when he gave his dying blessing to his grandsons Ephraim and Manasseh. It was an important moment. Jacob recognised that Joseph's sons stood in the line of succession to the covenant that God made with Abraham, and ratified to Isaac, and himself. It is also important because it shows us Jacob's mature reflection on a long life with more troubles than most men have. Look at Jacob's words in Genesis 48:15-16:

God, before whom my fathers, Abraham and Isaac
walked, the God who has fed me all my life long to this
day, the Angel who has redeemed me from all evil, bless
the lads; let my name be named upon them, and the
name of my fathers Abraham and Isaac; and let them
grow into a multitude in the midst of the earth.

The aged patriarch had reached the point where he could
recognise that God had dealt kindly with him. He understood,
and worshipped.

Faith is a plant that grows in the unpromising soil of the
human personality. It therefore needs severe pruning. Are we
like Jacob? Do we share his tendency to take things into our
own hands? Do we treat faith as a last resort, as though it were
intended for emergency use only? Jacob knew his strengths: he
was clever. His speed of thought meant that he could keep ahead
of his rivals. He deceived Esau, and later his uncle Laban, until
God confronted him with a situation that could not be resolved
by stealth. Jacob's life is a sad mixture of blessings and tragedy.
Jacob lived by trickery and it is not surprising that his sons
followed the example that he set. Later, when Shechem the
Hivite prince married Jacob's daughter Dinah, his sons Levi
and Simeon tricked Shechem's people into being circumcised,
and then killed them while they were recovering from the
surgery. Jacob himself became the victim of a cruel hoax when
his sons sold their brother Joseph into slavery and lied about
what had happened to him. Trouble came in other ways too.
His son Judah disgraced the family by committing incest with
his daughter-in-law Tamar. Rachel, the wife that he loved with
single-minded devotion, died in childbirth. As he summed up
his life when speaking to Pharaoh, Jacob said, *few and evil
have been the days of the years of my life* (Genesis 47:9).
Nevertheless, he was able to thank the one who had fed him all
his days and redeemed him *from all evil* (Genesis 48:15-16).

Some people say that their faith has never recovered because of some tragedy in their lives. The Hebrew Christians who first read this letter had faced great difficulties in the past, and saw more problems lying ahead. The author feared that they would conclude that God did not care for them. Let them think about Jacob, and what he endured! At the end of his life he was serene and calm because he understood why God had sent the trials. They were not meant to destroy his faith, but to stimulate it. Each trial helped him to rely not on himself but on God. Faith that has been heated in the furnace, and hammered on the anvil, is brighter and keener for it.

Faith tested by success (22)

Joseph is also introduced to us at the end of his life. He instructed his brothers that when the time came for the Israelite people to leave Egypt, he wanted them to exhume his bones and take them back to Canaan. He knew that God had promised a great future for the Hebrew people, in that land. They would not be in Egypt for ever. Their stay there was only temporary. Joseph wanted to make it clear whose side he was on. He wanted to identify himself with God's purpose, and God's people. He was not an Egyptian, and had no wish to leave his mortal remains in a land where he was a stranger. Nevertheless, the trial was real. He had lived in Egypt for many years and had become used to the land and its culture. His wife was Egyptian. He had wealth and position. No-one born outside the royal family could have done better. He could have had a tomb to rival that of Pharaoh, a gigantic mausoleum that would have caused slaves to toil for decades. How did he feel when his brothers arrived unexpectedly? They must have seemed coarse and uncivilised. Was he embarrassed by them? His Egyptian colleagues were repelled by Hebrew table manners. Would he lose credibility with them if he associated too closely with such unattractive primitives?

Material success is a hard trial to master. It introduces us to new circles. Christian friends seem uncultivated in comparison with our sophisticated new friends. Our taste may become too refined for simple godliness! The Hebrew Christians of the first century had to choose between the safe world of Judaism on the one hand, and being a despised sect on the other. Is it so different today? Sophisticated people regard Christian moral standards as throwbacks to a bygone age. Some people regard Christianity as a quick way to commit intellectual or social suicide. Joseph knew better. Faith saw a long way into the future, to a time when a despised gang of slaves would depart in triumph from a land grieving the slaughter of its firstborn. Joseph chose to identify with those slaves knowing they would eventually be victorious. How do you respond to the cause of Christ? Do you see it as a pathetic relic of days gone by, a historical curiosity? Or do you see a glorious future for it, a future so certain and secure that the world's view of 'success' no longer matters? That is the response of faith.

24
LESSONS IN FAITH FROM THE LIFE OF MOSES

Please read Hebrews 11:23-29

Introduction

The Bible is a practical book, and Hebrews 11 is one of the most practical chapters in it. It was originally written to help Jewish Christians face severe trials that had occurred because of their faith in Christ. It will help us too. The patriarch Moses is yet another example of a servant of God who faced a number of demanding situations. Five lessons follow.

1. The faith of Moses' parents (23)

The background to this story is the situation in Egypt a few decades before the Exodus. The Israelites were no longer the extended family of one man, but a people numerous enough to frighten their Egyptian hosts into attempting to suppress them. First of all, they forced all the Israelite men to work in the construction industry, and secondly an effort was made to destroy all male children at birth. This barbarous edict was in force when the infant Moses was born to Amram and Jochebed. God had given them a *beautiful child*. This does not just mean that he was an attractive baby. The martyr Stephen said that the child was 'well pleasing to God' (Acts 7:20). As parents, they naturally wanted to protect their own flesh and blood, but more than that, they knew that God had a special destiny for this child. They believed that great things lay in store, and took steps to preserve his life. This involved a fearful risk. We are told that *they were not afraid of the King's command.* We must not assume from this that they were oblivious to ordinary human feelings. Faith does not perform a strange kind of surgery on a person's emotions, and remove his capacity for worry, doubt, or in this case, fear. No, faith confronts these things and overcomes them.

In the event, the reward was out of all proportion to the faith. Moses was brought up in Pharaoh's court, the only place in Egypt where a Jewish boy would be safe. He had the benefit of his mother's nurture, while experiencing for himself the workings of the Egyptian monarchy. No doubt this was all to his advantage when the time came for him to confront Pharaoh face to face. Amram and Jochebed sensed that their child was special, but they could never have anticipated how much God would accomplish through him. Raising children is demanding work. So is teaching Sunday School, and Youth Work. Think of the potential! Charles Spurgeon was once a boy in Sunday School. God can do astonishing things with a single child.

2. Faith's choice (24-26)

There is a beautiful irony in the story of Moses. God raises up champions in the most unlikely surroundings. The Papacy has not yet recovered from the defeats inflicted on it by Martin Luther, a man who imbibed Roman Catholicism with his mother's milk. The most redoubtable foe of the Egyptian monarchy was educated in the palace. It is just like God to prepare his greatest heroes under the noses of his enemies! Moses owed much to the fact that his mother became his nurse. Her role in shaping his thinking cannot be underestimated. Eventually, he had to face a fateful decision. Where did his future lie? In Exodus 2:11-15 we learn that he killed an Egyptian whom he found beating a Hebrew. From now on there could be no turning back. There were two aspects to Moses' choice. First of all, he gave something up. He turned his back on his title, a secure future, wealth, and a position in the ruling elite of the most advanced civilisation of that age. The attractions of staying in Egypt were obvious, but this would mean siding with sin. His calling was to identify with the oppressed Hebrews. He had no mandate from God to stay where he was. In any case, Egypt could only offer temporary comfort. There was no future in it. God's plans lay elsewhere. The first century Hebrews faced a similar choice. They could remain on the side of Judaism, but this would mean clinging to a system that was obsolete. In the same way, the person who would follow Jesus must face a parting of the ways. The old life exerts a strong pull, but in the end, to live for ourselves is to refuse God his due. In other words, we cast our vote for the *pleasures of sin* (25).

In addition to rejecting his former life of rank and wealth, Moses chose a new direction. It brought upon him *the reproach of Christ* (26). Like Jesus, he found that the path of obedience to God led through a wilderness of misunderstanding and hostility. True faith will meet opposition! No disciple of Christ can claim that no one warned him about the trials ahead. When Jesus preached the gospel, he always advised those who wanted to be his disciples to count the cost. (Remember his parables about the man who set out to build a tower without the resources to see the job through, and the King who went to war without comparing his forces with those of his opponents. [Luke 14:28-32]). There is more to faith than a momentary emotional crisis. True faith weighs and calculates. What made Moses willing to leave polite society for the company of slaves covered in brick dust? What sustained him in the face of ridicule? He believed that the reproaches of God's enemies were a medal to be worn with honour. (You can tell a lot about a man by the kind of enemies he attracts). Furthermore, Moses *looked to the reward* (26). He knew that God is no man's debtor and that trials in the present were a necessary prelude to a glorious future. Faith knows that there must be endurance in this life, but it also knows that *the sufferings of this present time are not worthy to be compared with the glory which shall be revealed in us* (Romans 8:18). It is worth noting that this is not a way of persuading people to accept injustices in this life by promising them heaven in the next. Although Christians do look forward to a blessed eternity, there are also compensations in this life. Like the Psalmist, believers expect to *see the goodness of the Lord in the land of the living* (Psalm 27:13). The man who knows that he enjoys the approval of God is not easily deflected from his purpose.

3. Faith's endurance (27)

This verse refers to the first time Moses left Egypt, after he had killed the Egyptian. The account in Exodus explains that his first departure took place because he was frightened that Pharaoh would kill him, while here we read that he did not fear *the wrath of the King*. This can be resolved. Ordinarily, Moses does not seem to have lacked physical courage. He did not so much fear for his own safety, but for the effect that his death would have on his mission. Conscious of his task, he tried to hurry the Almighty along. His assault on the Egyptian was an attempt to rally the Israelites in a bid for freedom. It was premature. No one responded to his call. He had been precipitate. If he were caught and killed, there would be no second chance. That is what he was afraid of! He fled, and spent the next forty years learning to submit to God's sense of timing. (It is sobering to realise that God's plans for Israel were not concerned solely with Israel. In Gen 15:16 we learn of a prophecy that Israel would return to Canaan when the iniquity of the Amorites was full. She was to be God's instrument of judgement on the pagan nations). In the meantime, during forty long years in Sinai, Moses kept the vision alive. This is a lesson to Christians in every age. The Hebrew believers to whom this letter was addressed needed endurance. Modern Christians need staying power too. Few things discredit the gospel more than the kind of Christianity that does not last. Had we been given Moses' task, and received that initial setback, no doubt we would have sulked in the wilderness and given it up as a bad job. Moses' faith is a lesson in patience and staying power. His eyes were not fixed on the disappointments, but on the invisible God who called him on.

4. Faith's obedience (28)

The scene now changes. Forty years have passed. The Exodus of the whole nation of Israel was imminent. It is the occasion of the very first *Passover* celebration. Do we appreciate the enormity of Moses' task? First of all, he had to persuade the entire Hebrew nation to fall in with the message from God, and keep the ritual exactly as God had commanded. All the while, Moses knew that his credibility as leader was at stake. If things did not turn out as he predicted, his authority would evaporate. If the Egyptian firstborn survived, or if just one of the Israelite firstborn were to die, he would be discredited. He knew that he had raised the people's hopes of leaving Egypt. This was a nervous time for Moses. Would God let him down?

The lesson here is that faith is obedient. When God speaks, the person with faith does what the Almighty requires. Some preachers tell us that holy living is an option for the Christian.

As well as being untrue, this is nonsense. The person who says
he trusts God, but will not do as God says, is deceiving himself.
The first century Hebrew believers faced the temptation of choos-
ing the quiet life. Obedience had led them into difficulties.
Perhaps we feel that it was easier for Moses. God had spoken
to him: he had a plain path before him. This is a mistake on our
part. Our problem is not confusion, but courage. We know the
will of God as clearly as Moses did. The Bible is there before us.
Our problem is that we sense that obedience will exact a price,
and draw back from it. The two words 'Trust and Obey' can't
be separated. Those who will not obey do not trust.

5. Faith at the outer limits (29)

At this point the author invites us to picture the scene at the Red
Sea. The fleeing Israelites were an undisciplined rabble, seized
with panic as Pharaoh's cavalry came after them in hot pursuit.
Could an unarmed, untrained mob withstand professional
soldiers? There was no escape. Ahead lay the ocean. The scene
was set for a massacre. Now picture the dramatic moment when
the faith of one man kindled faith in the rest: *Stand and see the
salvation of the* LORD (Exodus 14:13). The people still needed
faith when the waters parted before their eyes. Would you not
think twice before walking on the sea bed with a wall of water
towering above you on either side? Could you be certain that
the whole mass of it would not come crashing down? Was God
playing with them? The only way of escape was to walk right
through the jaws of a watery death. They had to believe that
God would do as he had said. His power was terrifying. Could
they be sure of it? Would he use that awesome power to crush
them or to save them?

Note that God took sides. The power that took Israel to safety
dry shod, brought thousands of gallons of liquid destruction on

the Egyptians. This incident happened over 3,000 years ago, but it leaves us with something to ponder. According to the Bible, that same power will have a role to play in every human life. Ultimately, a similar fate lies in store for us all. Either God will save us, or he will destroy us. The difference is that it is not just our bodies that are at stake. One fate or the other is certain: eternal security *or* eternal ruin. Jesus bids us enter a narrow gate, and follow a steep and cramped pathway. At the end of it, life beckons. Some respond to his invitation, others do not. It is faith that distinguishes them. Do you have faith? It involves more than words. It begins with a decisive choice. It commits itself to a life of steady endurance. Faith is under orders, even when the situation is enough to make strong men tremble. Does this seem too much? Here is the key. You do not need mighty faith to win through, but faith in a mighty God.

25
FAITH AT JERICHO

Please read Hebrews 11:30-31

Introduction

Our journey through Hebrews 11 has been rather like a tour through a portrait gallery. One after another we have considered the lives of Old Testament characters who gained a good testimony because of their faith. The writer of Hebrews originally compiled these pen-portraits for the benefit of first century Jewish Christians, whose faith needed to be encouraged. It has been good for us too, for we are not much different to them. Now the time has come to consider the last case study in faith to be explored in detail. The author takes us back to the days of Joshua and the conquest of Canaan, and in particular the fall of Jericho, recorded in Joshua 6.

Faith and the work of God (30)

Once the Israelite people had crossed the Jordan, the city of Jericho demanded their attention (see Joshua 5:13-6:27). They could not afford to ignore it. It was a formidable military obstacle. Because of its position, it commanded the communications of the region. It covered both the East-West route across the Jordan, and the North-South route through the Judaean heartland. The Israelites would never be safe if Jericho was free to harry their communications. Furthermore, it was a difficult city to conquer, with impressive fortifications, a safe water supply, and sufficient stocks of food to withstand a long siege. The King of Jericho knew that the Israelites had no siege-engines, or battering rams. In most normal situations, lightly armed infantry would not be able to overcome a well-defended fortress.

At this point we pay tribute both to the faith of Joshua, and of the people of Israel. Jericho itself was a challenge to faith. It was in their path and they simply had to conquer it. The enemy city however, was not the only thing that called for faith. God himself had set them a daunting task. In Joshua 6 we are told that God showed Joshua that he wanted the campaign to be conducted in a very unconventional manner. No assault was to be mounted on the city at all. Indeed, the plan that God laid down would have had most military experts of the period frantic with worry. On each of six days, the people, led by the priests carrying the Ark of the Covenant, were to circle the city in complete silence. On the seventh day, they were to perform this action seven times, then the priests were to blow their trumpets and the people were to give a great shout. It was no more than a religious procession. If the defenders of Jericho were to mount a counter-attack and sally out of the city, the Israelites would be vulnerable in the extreme. Victory when it came owed nothing to Joshua, or to the people. It was God's triumph. The only part the Israelites played is that they were allowed to assist in destroying the people and animals of the city (Joshua 6:21).

The message is clear: God will honour his work, when it is done in his way. I wonder whether some of Joshua's commanders despaired of him: 'Do you have to be so pedantically biblical? This will never work you know!' Every generation of Christians faces a similar challenge. There is work to be done for God. In particular, we are required to take the gospel to the world. This often seems an impossible task. We must tell people that God looks upon them as sinners. No wonder they are prejudiced against our message from the outset! Then, in a world that values self-reliance, we are to call upon people to rely on God instead. Moreover, we are to use an unsophisticated method, so quaint that modern people smile at it. We are to preach. God demands that we talk to people. This involves formal preaching. It also involves being frank with people in everyday conversation. (Acts 8:4 tells us about one consequence of Saul's persecution of the Church. *Those who were scattered went every where preaching the word.* Obviously this does not refer to formal sermons. In this sense, ever believer is to be a preacher. We all have a duty to talk with others about the gospel.) Some believers however, appear to feel that evangelism cannot be so simple. Surely there is more to it than that? In any case, it will never work! It may have served the Puritans or the early Methodists well enough, but the world has changed. All around we can see those who concoct elaborate stratagems aimed at finding the right method for the current situation. In such a setting, the story of Jericho speaks to us down the centuries. Of course the world would do things differently, but however improbable it seemed beforehand, God brought the walls down. Our task is to do as we are told, confident that God will accomplish his purposes. Our duty is simply to talk to people! The world may write this off as a foolish approach, but then I expect the defenders of Jericho laughed as the Israelites made their circuit of the city. Let us not lose our nerve. The walls will crumble in due time.

Faith and the outsider (31)

We have seen what God did through the faith of Joshua and his companions, but we must never imagine that faith is something that only belongs to insiders. Certainly the bulk of those who served God in Old Testament days were Jews, but it would be a mistake to imagine that faith was the exclusive property of the Jewish race. Here and there in the Old Testament we come across examples of outsiders who lay a claim to the grace of Israel's God. One of these is Rahab the prostitute, a citizen of Jericho who hid the Israelite spies, and thus identified herself with the people of God.

It is significant that Rahab was a woman, the only woman in this catalogue of the heroes of faith, but many other women in the Old Testament pleased God because of their faith. There are many examples. Faith is not an exclusively male affair. There are certain religions where men seem to have an advantage over women. (Mormonism for instance teaches that husbands decide whether or not their wives deserve to be resurrected). During the time of Jesus' ministry, his attitude to women marked him out as being very different from the normal rabbis of that age. Mary Magdalene, and the woman of Samaria had both led wicked lives, but Jesus accepted them. There is neither male nor female in Christ (Gal 3:28). Women may enter the kingdom of heaven on the same terms as men. Leave off sinning, have faith in Christ and you will be welcome.

Rahab was also a person with a guilty past. Until she became a servant of the Lord, she earned her living as a prostitute. Some people suppose that the life of faith is only open to conformists. When Christianity was fashionable, churches tended to attract 'respectable' people. Ordinary folk felt excluded because churchgoers behaved as though they were morally superior to everyone else. Would women like Rahab find a welcome in today's churches? There is no doubt where Jesus stood with regard to such people. His parable about the prodigal son (Luke 15:11-32) is very helpful. The prodigal son is a recognisable type: the rebel who threw himself into a life of pleasure seeking. Let us not forget the other character in the parable: the older brother, a conformist who never did anything wrong. Behind the respectable facade however, there was an attitude problem. He was proud of his responsible and respectable life. In one respect the prodigal was wiser than his older brother. The prodigal faced up to his guilt. Jesus often encountered the 'older brother syndrome' among the Pharisees (see Matthew 21:31-32). In the days of the early church, people like Rahab were not uncommon. Look at 1 Cor 6:9-11.

> Do you not know that the unrighteous will not inherit the kingdom of God? Do not be deceived. Neither fornicators, nor idolaters, nor adulterers, nor homosexuals, nor sodomites, nor thieves, nor covetous, nor drunkards, nor revilers, nor extortioners will inherit the kingdom of God. And such were some of you. But you were washed, but you were sanctified, but you were justified in the name of the Lord Jesus and by the Spirit of our God.

It is clear from the apostle Paul's words here that the church at Corinth contained a number of people who, before their conversion, had lived in ways that were very displeasing to God. Have you ever felt that faith is not for you, because of something that you've done? Are there moral failures in your past? Rahab, and many more, remind us that God is the God of new beginnings. Jesus became notorious because he accepted tax collectors and sinners. He still does. At the same time, there must be a willingness to have done with sin. (I recently heard an interview on the Radio where a practising homosexual complained that the church would not accept people like him. He maintained that Jesus did. He had evidently forgotten Jesus' words to the woman caught in the act of adultery: *'Go, and sin no more'* [John 8:11]).

Rahab was also a foreigner. There have always been people who have looked on the Church from the outside, feeling that they did not belong. It was never intended that the Church should be a club for 'people like us'. Of course there can be tensions. In the book of Acts we see Christians of Jewish extraction having to make adjustments for the sake of new-comers from a variety of Gentile backgrounds. No doubt it took a lot of grace to overcome deep-seated prejudice on the one hand, or unintended thoughtlessness on the other. Are you being held back from discipleship because you feel that you have to be a certain type of person to thrive in Christian circles? Have you ever excused yourself by saying, 'I am not the religious type'? Surely Rahab is a reminder that the grace of God has a welcome for the outsider! Faith is not the exclusive property of certain privileged groups. In this respect, Rahab set a very important precedent. The genealogy in Matthew 1:5 tells us that she married a man named Salmon. They had a son called Boaz, who also married a foreigner, Ruth the girl from Moab. With his background, he could hardly object to marrying a girl from gentile stock! In the course of time, King David, and Jesus himself were descended from a prostitute and a foreigner who found grace in the sight of God.

Faith in the God who reveals himself

I have heard people say that faith is 'a leap in the dark'. They make Christian commitment sound like a guessing game. Rahab's story proves that it is not! Rahab's faith was based on knowledge. It is clear from the account in Joshua 2:9-11 that she understood something of the power of God. She had followed the story of Israel's journey out of Egypt with avid interest. It was clear that no one could stand against them. Yahweh was a formidable adversary. Several kings had fallen already, and she knew what would happen to the foolish King of Jericho who was preparing himself to stand in the path of this awesome God. On the other hand, it was clear that such a

God as this was well able to protect his own. To provoke his anger was very foolish, but an appeal to his mercy would show just how generous he could be. Nothing has changed. We must all encounter that same God one day. We know from the Bible what kind of God he is, combining *goodness and severity* (Romans 11:22). We commend him to you on the basis of what you can know and experience. Since everyone must meet him, is it not wise to come to terms with him while there is time for mercy? Rahab knew that if she did not act soon, the time would come when the opportunity to seek Yahweh's protection would have passed. Look at Psalm 2:12. Our position is that we are rebels against a great God. All is not lost. Blessedness is possible, but only for those who will make their peace with Messiah. There is a real danger that if we delay too long, we will have to endure the whole weight of his indignation. Why wait a moment longer?

26

THE RACE OF FAITH

Please read Hebrews 11:32-12:2

Introduction

And what more shall I say? It is clear from this remark in verse 32 that the author faced a problem. There was a lot more that could be said! The subject of faith had not been exhausted. The Old Testament Scriptures contained many similar cases to those he had already mentioned. Nevertheless, time was short, and he had given his readers, then and now, many stirring examples to stimulate their faith. The time had come to complete this section of the letter, and bring it to a conclusion.

The achievements of faith (32-35a)

The author could have listed all the men and women of faith in the Old Testament. Instead, he ends his catalogue by referring to certain characters who lived in the days of the Judges, and the earliest days of the Israelite monarchy. The people mentioned by name in verse 32 all have something in common. Each one accomplished extraordinary things by faith. Gideon risked his life by throwing down a monument to the pagan god Baal, and also achieved a remarkable military victory against the Midianites with a lightly armed contingent of 300 men

(Judges 6:11-8:35). Barak's infantry triumphed against the Canaanite general Sisera, whose cavalry was equipped with iron chariots, the most advanced military technology available at that time (Judges 4:1-24). Samson secured many spectacular triumphs, the most notable in his dying moments, when he pulled the Temple of Dagon down on the heads of his Philistine captors (Judges 13:1-16:31). Jephthah, a comparative nobody, rescued his people from oppression by the Ammonites (Judges 11:1-12:7). David's story, from the killing of Goliath onward, is a string of glorious achievements. Samuel, during a long ministry, changed the moral tone of a whole people. In vv.33-35 we also have a list of remarkable events, each one accomplished through faith. No one is mentioned by name, but it is not hard to work out who is intended.

None of the men named in verse 32 was perfect. Each had his share of human failings. Gideon's courage could be uncertain and his pleas for unmistakable signs from God betrayed a very weak faith indeed. Barak refused to go into battle without the help of the prophetess, Deborah. Samson's life swung like a pendulum between extremes of greatness and monumental weakness. Jephthah made a foolish vow, David's domestic life was a mess, and even the wise Samuel repeated the mistake of his mentor Eli, and failed to discipline his sons. We can take courage from this. As we look back on our lives, we may regret a great deal, but none of our past failures disqualifies us from doing something for God. The main element in the stories of these characters is that when God called, each one responded. The achievements of faith do not depend on faith itself. Jesus said that a quantity of faith no greater than a mustard seed would do. Faith works wonders only when it leans upon a wonder-working God.

The sufferings of faith (35b-40)

Over the years, many Christians have thanked God for the author's pastoral wisdom in including these verses. Not everyone can identify with the triumphant note of the earlier verses. How many of us can say that our faith has been rewarded with such amazing successes as subduing kingdoms and stopping the mouths of lions? What we are given here is the other side of the story. The catalogue of triumphs that we have already considered is now matched by a catalogue of sufferings. Some of the incidents mentioned here are drawn from the lives of the prophets, others from the persecution of faithful Jews during the period of the Maccabees. Verse 35 speaks of torture. This refers to being stretched, as upon a rack, and then beaten. Imprisonment is mentioned in verse 36. This was the fate of Jeremiah on two occasions. Moreover, an ancient tradition says that he died by stoning in Egypt. Certainly Jesus once said that Jerusalem was the city which stoned the messengers of God (Matthew 23:37)! According to another tradition, Isaiah was murdered during the reign of the evil King Manasseh by being sawn in two. What a horrible list of persecutions! Taken together they illustrate a sad fact: the world's scale of values is upside down. Those people who most deserve its respect, are often treated with casual barbarity.

These verses remind us of something that we easily forget. We tend to think that the will of God is something that we do. While this is often the case, there are also times when the will of God must be borne. As far as the first readers of the Epistle were concerned, the will of God meant enduring persecution. God called the Apostle Paul to serve him with a physical ailment so inhibiting that he called it a *thorn in the flesh* and a *messenger of Satan* (2 Corinthians 12:7). Joni Eareckson is an American lady who broke her neck in a swimming accident at the age of eighteen. She was paralysed from the shoulders downwards. God's plan for her is that she should live the Spirit-filled life, in a wheelchair. It may be the will of God for you or me to live for his glory while carrying a burden. This may be the hostility of others to the gospel that we love, or any one of a vast number of things: poor health, financial stringency, responsibility to a sick loved one, a job that we dislike but can't change, and more besides. We often suppose that such burdens prevent us from serving God. In point of fact, these are the very situations where he wants us to serve him. We must prove God where we are. (We may never have the chance to prove him where we would like to be). John Wesley understood this very well when he drafted the Methodist Covenant Service, with its prayer, 'Put me to doing; put me to suffering'. Whether it is our task to do things for the Lord, or to bear his will patiently, we need the same faith. Indeed, the faith that steadfastly endures can be greatly effective as a witness to God's grace. Many a person has been won for Christ by the calm trust of a friend in adversity.

Some might say that God played a cruel joke on these people. A life spent trusting him ended in violent and painful death. Had the Almighty cheated them? The answer is in vv. 39-40. These verses focus on the word *perfect*. This takes us back to the argument earlier in the Epistle that Judaism was a preparatory religion. Imperfect prophets and priests, sacrifices that could never take away sins, a temple that would pass away, and a covenant that human beings could not keep were meant to pave the way for something perfect. Once Jesus had come, these things had served their purpose. The suffering believers mentioned in this passage lived at a time when this had not yet happened. Their faith looked forward to a Messiah who was promised, but had not yet come. Our faith looks back to a Messiah who has come. Nevertheless, the object of our faith is one and the same. We see Jesus revealed in the written word of the New Testament, they glimpsed him by the dim light of prophecy and symbol. We and they live either side of that great watershed, the incarnation of the Son of God. Nevertheless, the way to God in every age is one and the same: we are justified through faith in Christ. We must learn from the example of these Old Testament saints. They achieved so much, endured so much, and suffered so much without the measure of gospel light that we enjoy. From those *to whom much is given...much shall be required* (Luke 12:48). In any case, we too await the fulfilment of certain promises. The grand culmination of God's purposes still lies in the future. The Church still needs those who can live by faith confident that whatever happens in the here and now, the best is yet to come.

The goal of faith (12:1-2)

At this point the focus changes. We have thought about the heroes of faith who lived long ago. In the light of all that they did and suffered, what about ourselves? At this stage the author uses an illustration that would be familiar to his first readers, the Games. The popularity of Greek culture meant that the practice of holding regular games festivals had spread throughout the Middle East. At that time, there were certain significant differences in the way that these competitions were organised compared with the modern approach. When races were held, the judges sat behind the finishing line. These were always distinguished former competitors. In addition, prizes were not awarded until the end of the whole festival. This meant that competitors from the later events watched those who went first. They in their turn, when their events were over, sat in the stands and cheered on those who came later.

The life of faith is like a race, and we are not the first to attempt it. There is a *cloud of witnesses* (1). The main idea here is not that they are watching us. The word translated 'witness' does not primarily mean spectator, as it does nowadays. The same word is sometimes translated 'martyr'. A martyr is a witness in the sense that he gives his life for the sake of the truth. It is not so much that the witnesses are watching us but rather that we have had the privilege of watching them. We have had the inspiration of seeing how they tackled the race. My grandfather served years ago in a regiment in the British Army known as the Durham Light Infantry. As is the case with many British regiments, its heritage acted as a spur to those who inherited it. It was no commonplace thing to know that your regimental motto, 'Faithful', was bestowed by no less a man than the Duke of Wellington, when the regiment was known as the 68th Foot, and that a long line of battle honours stretched back over two centuries. Men who served in the Durhams felt that they had to be worthy of their ancestors. During the Second World War, the Durhams were part of the allied force that invaded German occupied Sicily. A century and a half after Wellington's day, another great British general, Montgomery, declared that they were as 'steady as a rock'. They had proved as steady and reliable as their ancestors. We Christians have a heritage greater than any other. Over the years, that cloud of witnesses has grown as fresh generations have kept the faith. Pause for a moment as you run, and look at the vast stadium, packed with those who have gone before. The Old Testament saints are there, and I can see the martyrs of the early Church too. Is that Martin Luther? I see several rows of Huguenots, and rank upon rank of sober Scots Covenanters, and an English face or two: Cranmer, Tyndale, Bunyan, Wesley, Whitefield and many more. Among them are many unknown to history who lived in obscurity. Most nations of the world are represented. The witnesses urge us on: 'we kept the faith, we endured. Go and do the same!'

There is practical advice here. The Greek word 'gymnasium' comes from the verb 'to strip'. Everyday clothing was voluminous, so athletes competed naked. This explains the author's exhortation that we should *lay aside every weight and the sin which so easily ensnares us* (1). We won't run well if we are impeded by sin. It is like a garment that threatens to envelop us. Drop it! In particular, let us leave behind that sin of unbelief. Nothing clings to an athlete's feet quite so stubbornly. Furthermore, let us *run with endurance*, with dogged perseverance. Some Christians are easily beaten. Whether it is personal Bible Study, attending the Prayer Meeting, witnessing to friends, loving their fellow believers, or helping in some aspect of ministry, when they meet some minor obstacles they give up. At this point we would do well to reflect on the apostle Paul's words in Philippians 3:13-14.

> Brethren, I do not count myself to have apprehended; but one thing I do, forgetting those things which are behind and reaching forward to those things which are ahead, I press towards the goal for the prize of the upward call of God in Christ Jesus.

The section closes with the best incentive of all. In addition to the great 'cloud of witnesses', someone else has run the race before us. Look ahead! See who waits at the finishing post! He is the *author* of our faith as he is also the *finisher of our faith* (2); he has pioneered the way. He knows the cost of faith in God, he knows that endurance is won through affliction. The Cross and the shame were the background to his life of faith. Ahead of him lay the joy of his Father. Joy beckons us too. The one who pioneered the path of faith waits at the finishing line. He himself is the prize. *Run in such a way that you may obtain it!* (1 Corinthians 9:24).

27
A FATHER'S DISCIPLINE

Please read Hebrews 12:3-13

Introduction

Christians have many things in common. In the first place, they share the grace of God in Christ. It does not stop there, however. Believers also share, to a greater or lesser extent, the experience of tribulation. The Christian life is demanding. Some teachers claim that the opposite is true, that believers ought to enjoy a life of uninterrupted success, good health, and material prosperity. This kind of teaching is seductive; it appeals to our lower instincts. It is also an insult to the memory of the Hebrew believers who first received this Epistle. They went through *'a great struggle with sufferings'* for the sake of the gospel, including reproach and the destruction of their property (10:32-34). The 'Health and Wealth' gospel is also a slur on the memory of countless great saints of years gone by, for it suggests that the sufferings that they bore with fortitude need never have happened if they had only realised the secret of Christian success! We must realise that there is no easy way out, and there never has been. The Bible pictures the life of faith as something strenuous, at times even dangerous: it is a pilgrimage along a steep and rugged pathway, a race that demands strength and perseverance, a fight to the finish with a ruthless enemy. In the light of all this, the passage before us is immensely practical. It will help us prepare ourselves for the struggle.

Rough handling by a loving father

This portion of the Epistle includes a number of illustrations taken from the world of Sport. In vv.1-2 the Christian life is compared to a race. This idea is still to the fore in verse 3 where the author sets out to encourage those of his readers who might have become *weary and discouraged* in their souls, like runners faint with exhaustion who might be tempted to give up. Another echo of the ancient Greek games is found in verse 4 where the believer's struggle against sin is compared with the boxing ring. From verse 5 however, the scene changes. Instead of being compared to an athlete in the arena, the believer is described as a son being *trained* (11) by a loving father who understands that his children need to face a measure of hardship if they are to develop Christian character. Athletes know that muscles are built by subjecting them to stress. That is why people train with weights. Indeed, in most sports, those who take training seriously often 'put themselves through it'. It is arduous. It involves going through what sportsmen call 'the pain barrier'. In the same way, life in the Father's house has painful moments. The author's point is that the difficulties we experience in life are not merely random occurrences but the *chastening* that is inevitable in any well-ordered family. Even though the context is that of a parent's love, the discipline can be severe. Sometimes the pain is so acute, that the word *grievous* (11) fits it exactly. It is like being scourged (6). We need to appreciate the healthy realism of Scripture at this point. There is nothing pleasant about chastisement. We can bear it because we know that *afterwards it yields the peaceable fruit of righteousness to those who have been trained by it* (11). The apostle James writes as follows:

My brethren, count it all joy when you fall into various trials, knowing that the testing of your faith produces patience. (James 1:2-3).

These words make the same point as our passage from Hebrews. This is important because some believers have mis-understood James' emphasis on joy. The result is that they try to keep a joyful expression on their faces when they feel devas-tated. It is artificial; they are pretending. Tribulation is not a joyous thing, and it is not necessarily ungodly to feel sad or upset. Job lost ten sons. Peter and John were flogged. These were horrid experiences. If God's chastisement for you or me should involve persecution, physical pain, ill health, debility, bereavement, unemployment, poverty, or anything else, the distress is real. Joy comes when we take the long-term view, and keep the outcome in mind. The message of this passage is like the advice of a wise parent giving unpleasant medicine to a child: 'I know it tastes nasty, but it will do you good'.

The wrong response to the treatment

Some Christians receive chastisement from God, and are no better for it, because they adopt the wrong attitude. Two such attitudes are outlined in verse 5. In the first place, we must not *despise the chastening of the Lord*. In other words, we must not take things lightly and assume that the hand of God is not behind whatever has happened to us. Even believers of long standing can be guilty of this. Something happens to us, and we shrug our shoulders and say that it is nothing more than coincidence. This often happens because we confuse chastise-ment with punishment. We imagine that the adverse events in life are specific punishments for particular sins. In consequence, when we know that we have sinned we can be terrified, won-dering just how God is going to 'get even' with us in the next few days. Equally, if we are not conscious of sin, we conclude that since we are not to blame, that what has happened is sheer bad luck. This way of thinking has two fatal flaws in it. First of all, our sin is so offensive to God that if he did punish us in the here and now, that punishment would be far worse than the mere ups and downs of life. Secondly, God punished your sin and mine at Calvary. He has no need to settle accounts with us in this life because our sin has already been punished in full. Chastisement is not punishment, but discipline. Certain obstacles are placed in our path. As we learn to overcome them, we grow. God knows us well. He concentrates on our weak spots. Next time we find ourselves under discipline, our response ought to be to ask ourselves what lesson we are being taught, so that God does not need to treat us in the same way again.

The other wrong attitude is to become *discouraged*, to faint and become weary in spirit. Some people are especially prone to this, indeed most of us probably react like this at one time or another. This was the Hebrews' problem. They had grown tired, and felt like giving up. It is the mentality that says things like, 'Oh what's the good? It never gets any better! What's the point? Why do we have to go through all this?' Those who give way to this kind of thinking soon end up wallowing in bitterness and self-pity. We easily forget that God loves us too much to leave us as we are. We are not fit for heaven yet. The treatment is not over.

The correct response to the treatment

How should we respond to the chastisement of God? Look at vv.3-4. In these verses we are encouraged to get things in proportion. Unlike others, we have not been required to shed our blood in the struggle *against sin*. (The illustration here is taken from the boxing ring. Boxers in the Greek games used heavy metal gloves, which caused awful wounds). In Chapter 11 we considered those who *obtained a good testimony* (11:2) because their faith enabled them to surmount the challenges that they faced in days gone by. Can we really say that we have been called upon to suffer as the great martyrs of the faith did in earlier generations? But if there is much to be gained from studying the great *cloud of witnesses* (12:1) Jesus surely provides the ultimate example. In verse 3 we are encouraged to *consider* the way that he endured the malice of those who opposed him. Have we endured anything as daunting as the opposition that Jesus faced?

Furthermore, our passage directs us to the best remedy of all. We need to remind ourselves that God is our Father. This is the message of verse 7. The main point of the verse is that we do not suffer at random. Our sufferings are the discipline of a loving father. God is dealing with us as sons. The Hebrews ought to have known this. Verses 5 and 6 are a quotation taken from the Old Testament Scriptures, from Proverbs 3:11-12. What else do you expect from a father? What kind of parent never disciplines his children? Christians who resent God's discipline are behaving exactly as small children do. It is only as we get older that we begin to understand what our parents meant when they told us that they punished us because they loved us! They had the future in mind. They didn't want us to grow up to be spoiled. As we look back we no doubt have rueful memories of occasions when our parents overdid the punishment or spanked the innocent child instead of the ringleader. Perhaps there were times when they were under strain and shouted at us for no good reason. Nevertheless, we learned to take it philosophically because we grew to see that on the whole they did what they did out of love for us. We are no better, and can only hope that our children will forgive our bouts of bad temper and inconsistency.

God is so much greater than our natural fathers. He is never tired, or irritable, cruel or vindictive. He never lashes out, or does anything thoughtlessly. He is not capricious. He never overdoes it! (Does it seem as though the trial will never stop?)

All that happens to us comes from the heart of one who loves us more than tongue can tell. Verse 9 tells us that we should submit to the treatment, recognising the love that motivates it. Think about it! Some people seem to get off lightly. Is it possible that they are not truly children of this gracious father whose tender love will not let us languish in mediocrity?

The essential thing in physical training is that we keep it up. When muscles begin to ache we tend to nurse them to minimise the pain. The best remedy for cramped limbs is to set them in motion again. That explains the encouragement of vv.12-13. Stiffen your spine, recapture the spring in your stride. When the chastening comes, do not be tempted to discount it, or ignore it, but seek the face of God in it!

28
A FINAL CALL TO PERSEVERE

Please read Hebrews 12:14-29

Introduction (14)

The Epistle to the Hebrews is a sustained challenge to Christian people to persevere in the faith that they profess. These verses, which form the concluding part of the doctrinal section of the Epistle, teach this theme for the last time. Once again, the author calls upon his readers to go on, and not to turn back. This explains the opening statement in verse 14. The Jewish believers who first received this letter had made enemies because of their faith in Christ. Human beings either try to avoid their enemies, or seek to destroy them. By contrast, the Hebrews were to live at *peace with all men*, patiently seeking to absorb the malice of their opponents. Meekness is not coward-ice. They must not return evil for evil, but they were not to quit the fight. At the same time, they were also to *pursue ... holiness*. This was a challenge to believers tempted to fall into spir-itual mediocrity. It seemed that devotion to Christ had brought nothing but trouble. The idea that salvation and blessing could be gained without the burdensome challenge of holy living seemed very attractive. This attitude is still with us. Do we really have to live holy lives? Would it not be enough to get by with the minimum? Political parties and Trade Unions have ordinary members who just pay their subscriptions and turn up at the Annual General Meeting on the one hand, and enthusiasts on the other, but this mentality will not do in the Christian Church. Holiness is an absolute necessity. No one may see the Lord without it. It is the only solid proof that a person is the Christian that he claims to be. Are we holy?

The root of bitterness (15-17)

Verse 15 is not a caution against bitterness in general. There is no doubt that a bitter spirit has a corrosive effect on a Christian, and the Bible has much to say about this elsewhere. At this point however, the author advises us to beware of a particular kind of person. (It is not unusual for a person to be called a *root* in the Bible; Jesus himself is described in that way in Isaiah 11). Churches should be on the alert. If certain people are left undisturbed, a bitter harvest will follow. It all becomes clear when we realise that the author is quoting from the Old Testament. Look at Deuteronomy 29:18-19.

> So that there may not be among you man or woman or family or tribe, whose heart turns away today from the LORD our God, to go and serve the gods of these nations, and that there may not be among you a root bearing bitterness or wormwood; and so it may not happen, when he hears the words of this curse, that he blesses himself in his heart, saying, 'I shall have peace, even though I walk in the imagination of my heart' – as though the drunkard could be included with the sober.

These verses take us back to the time when the Israelites were about to enter the Promised Land. The people had entered into a solemn covenant with God. This had been accompanied by a number of gracious promises, and a series of sombre warnings. The *root bearing bitterness* describes the kind of person who, in his heart of hearts, treats the whole exercise with contempt. While he mixes with true believers and may seem outwardly to be one of them, his state of mind is not that of a genuine Christian. His outward behaviour may be respectable enough to convince some observers that he is a follower of Jesus but within himself there is a stubborn refusal to submit to God and his ways. Even though he puts on a convincing act, this person *falls short of the grace of God* (15).

Esau was that kind of person. In verse 16 we read of the way that he surrendered his birthright to his brother Jacob for a bowl of lentil stew. When it is put as simply as that, the sheer folly of it stands out. Certainly Esau was hungry, but to throw away his whole future for the sake of a full belly was criminal. His family inheritance was at risk, as was God's promised blessing on the descendants of his grandfather Abraham. Esau treated all that with contempt. He thought only of the moment. First century readers of this Epistle would see the relevance of this immediately. Would they do as Esau did, and lose the blessing that lay ahead in order to spare themselves a little hardship in the present? Our situation is no different. If we shrink back when the decisive moment comes, we say, in effect, that we are content to trade future blessing for present comfort. In Esau's case, the root produced a crop of bitter fruit. God would not relent (17). Esau's tears of misery and frustration had no effect. It was too late. There is a sombre warning here for those who claim to be Christians, but who tell themselves that it won't matter if they behave as they please. If you go on like that, one day you will be sorry.

People like that are a danger to others beside themselves. There is the danger that *many* will *become defiled* (15). This is why the image of the *root* is so apt. I once planted some mint root in my garden. Some months later, it had spread so widely that I had to uproot yards of soil to reach it. In any local church, the spiritual state of each member is the proper concern of everyone else. We cannot afford to have people among us who claim to be children of God, yet do not live as Christians ought to live. Their example will be contagious. For the sake of the whole Church, we must not merely make progress ourselves. We should take our share of responsibility for the progress of others too.

Two mountains (18-25)

The Epistle to the Hebrews compares two religions, Judaism and Christianity. God ordained both of them, but one was incomplete and provisional while the other was complete and permanent. The old was preparatory; the new concluded what the old had only begun. We now return to this comparison for the last time. In this passage, each religion is represented by a mountain: Judaism by the physical Mount Sinai, and Christianity by the spiritual Mount Zion, *heavenly Jerusalem* (22). There is no doubt which of the two mountains was the greater. An impressive, but forbidding portrait of Mount Sinai is given in vv.18-21. The fury of the elements, the flames and smoke, made it clear that Yahweh was not a God who could be ignored. Everything combined to tell the onlookers to keep back. When animals strayed onto the slopes, no one could follow them. They had to be killed at a distance, with missiles. Even Moses, who talked with God face to face, was clearly affected. Mount Zion however, is very different. The description is thrilling. Who would not wish to make his home among the myriads of angels? Who would not wish to have his citizenship among the firstborn? *God, the judge of all* (23) is content to have the *spirits of just men* surround him. The crucial point is that this mountain is also the home of *Jesus, the mediator of the new covenant* (24). His blood has provided the perfect sacrifice for sin that Judaism failed to provide. That is why it *speaks better things* (24) than the blood of Abel. Abel's blood, the first human blood to be shed, like the blood of Jesus, was that of an innocent victim. Nevertheless, it called out for vengeance. Jesus' blood tells us instead that vengeance has been satisfied. It speaks of an offended God who has been placated. It does not warn us to keep our distance, but tells us that we may come, and welcome.

Why does the author offer this comparison? The answer is given in verse 25. Some people refused the message of God when it was delivered from the earthly mountain. These are the ones described in Deuteronomy 29:19. They heard the message God sent through Moses. They received the offers of blessing, and heard the warnings. Nevertheless, their response was only superficial. Multitudes of them remained in the wilderness because the way ahead seemed too demanding. They never entered the rest that God had prepared. If that was the fate of those who would not obey under the old scheme of things, what excuse is available now that God speaks through his Son? The people who closed their ears to God when he spoke from the threatening slopes of Mount Sinai were very foolish. It is even more foolish to close our ears to God when he speaks from the gentle and welcoming slopes of Mount Zion. The new revelation is clear, and its message is inviting. It tells us that because Jesus has bled and suffered, we may be at peace with God. The Almighty condescends to plead with us (See Matthew 11:28-30). At the same time, we are told that those who come to Jesus for rest must bear his yoke. We are called to a life of service and self-denial. Every true believer has his occasional reverses, but what are we to conclude about those who never seem to make any progress? What about those who stagnate? They have a point to prove.

> Beware brethren, lest there be in any of you an evil heart of unbelief in departing from the living God; but exhort one another daily ... lest any of you be hardened through the deceitfulness of sin (3:12-13). 'How shall we escape if we neglect so great a salvation?' (2:3)

Two destinies (26-29)

Note once more the solemn warning of verse 25: *See that you do not refuse him who speaks*. We must persevere. The closing verses of chapter 12 remind us that we must not be short-sighted. This was Esau's problem. He thought no further than the gnawing hunger in in his stomach. The long-term consequences of his behaviour hardly seemed to matter at all. The first readers of this Epistle faced the same danger. Their immediate problem was persecution. The Jewish world had turned against them. Times were hard. Things were going badly. Naturally, they wanted an end to the torment. It was tempting to think that the pain could soon be over, if they would only compromise. Twenty centuries later, the same pressure is still there. It is fatally easy to behave as though we only had this world to contend with. After all, it is real and tangible. Our desire for material well being, creature comforts, and the good opinion of our fellow men weighs heavily upon us. We need to pause and give serious thought to the message of these verses, namely that there is nothing permanent about the present order of things.

Verse 26 points us back to Mount Sinai and tells us to remember the awesome earthquake that took place. Next we are told that this is only a pale shadow of another shaking, which lies ahead. The various cataclysms of nature will be as nothing compared to the events of that day. Before us lies the dissolution of all things. God will undo and remake not only the earth, but heaven also. Those who build all their hopes on this world and what it can offer are engaged in building a house of cards. The structure is flimsy. It will not last. Where is the wisdom of devoting energy and resources to something that is doomed to destruction? John Wesley had the true perspective. When he visited the magnificent homes of the aristocracy and observed all the costly furnishings he was sometimes tempted to feel envious of such wealth and comfort so he used to write in his diary, 'It will all burn up one day!' There are people who lose their hope of eternal happiness for the sake of some transient benefit in the here and now. That kind of thing is both short-sighted, and fundamentally stupid. Don't be like Esau! Don't leave yourself weeping helplessly over a day of grace passed and gone.

The author counsels us to build our future on something permanent. There is something that cannot be shaken. It is so solid that the holocaust of God's wrath will leave it unscathed. If only we had eyes to see it towering above the wreckage of a broken world! There is a Kingdom that will outlast every earthly kingdom, and indeed the very planet itself. This sin-sick world will sink in ruin, but the Kingdom of Christ, like a mighty rock, will be untouched by the storm of judgement. It is the inheritance of the people of God. Under the benevolent headship of the King of Kings, they will reign in it, and rule over it. A golden future beckons. Christian, this is your birthright! Is it really worth throwing it away for the sake of some trivial earthly blessing? With Esau, it was a bowl of soup. With others it might have been nothing more than a trifling promotion at work, or peace in the face of a nagging wife. Think it through. On the one hand, there is the possibility of service in the kingdom that nothing can destroy. On the other hand, there is something so bad that nothing could possibly be worse. Those who depart from the living God will have to face him one day. Hell is not a terror because the damned are there, or even because Satan is there. The horror of it lies in the fact that those who are sent there must meet God himself. Since they have despised his offer of mercy, and think so lightly of the blood of Jesus, nothing remains but the consuming fire of justice. No fate could be worse than to receive what we deserve!

29

THE NUTS AND BOLTS OF PERSEVERANCE

Please read Hebrews 13:1-17

Introduction

Do you ever write letters? Would you agree that it can be hard to bring them to a nice neat ending? You've written 'Yours Faithfully', but all manner of things come into your mind, and you end up with a load of PSs. Is this what we have in Hebrews 13? Did the author jot down a jumble of unconnected and random thoughts, having suddenly remembered that he had not put them in earlier? Actually, this is not just a chapter of bits and pieces. We have two series of directives. The first concerns the way that Christians ought to live in the world. The second concerns the spiritual side of life. Each exhortation is carefully chosen. The Hebrew believers who first read this letter would have been amazed at the way that these directives spoke directly to their situation. Here was a group of believers grappling with the temptation to slip back. All the way through the epistle the author has urged them to press on. Look at 10:21-23. These words sum up the thrust of his message. They have every reason to persevere. They have Jesus, a great High Priest. Going on the faith is worthwhile for his sake. Nevertheless, a question arises. Yes, believers must persevere, but how is this to be done? Are there any practical guidelines? This concerns us too. Twenty centuries may have passed, but the human heart has not changed. Christians are still prone to slip back, and the challenge to press on still confronts the believer.

Persevering in the things that we do (1-6)

These verses are very practical. They address questions that we face every day of the week. How do we react to the people in our lives, including our fellow believers? How do we handle the precious gift of sexuality? What is our attitude to material wealth? Even so, the author did not write these verses at random. There is a strong connection that links the different statements. The Hebrew believers had once been strong in these areas of Christian conduct, but in time they had grown weak. How sad that they had to be spoken to about *brotherly love* (1), for at one time they had stood by their brothers and sisters at some cost to themselves. Things were different now, for they had to be told not to give up coming together in fellowship (10:25). The author himself had known their practical kindness when he languished in gaol (10:34), yet now it was necessary to prompt them to have pity on those in prison (3). The challenge to be hospitable fits in to the same pattern. Here were people who had begun to lie low and keep themselves to themselves. The modern backslider is prey to the same symptoms. Do your brothers and sisters in Christ no longer seem attractive to you? Do you want less and less to do with them? Perhaps they are pathetic specimens, but is it just possible that the real reason why you feel this way is that your faith is less fervent than it used to be?

Why did the author mention marriage in verse 4? Believers stand out sharply from the world because they have a different attitude to sex. In the first century this took two forms. On the one hand, some religious cults were obsessed with virginity. Sex was unclean. You could only be truly spiritual if you were celibate. This attitude lingers on in Roman Catholicism. Clergy, and those in religious orders, must be protected from defilement. Over against this the Bible affirms that the marriage bed is not defiled, but honourable. On the other hand, there was no shortage of people at that time who took the view that everyone should have as much sexual activity as they wanted. This idea is common today. Sex is regarded as a kind of sport. At this point we see the wonderful balance and sanity of Scripture. Sex is a gift of God, to be enjoyed with thanksgiving. It is a wholesome, even a godly thing for married couples to enjoy physical love, but this is only permitted within the married relationship. All forms of sexual activity outside of marriage, whether heterosexual or homosexual, are forbidden. They are detestable in the sight of God, and those who practise these things will have to reckon with his judgement. A sure sign that a believer's faith has begun to degenerate is that he has begun to allow himself to think indulgently about things that he would once have condemned outright. It is an unusual Christian man who does not struggle, at least in his younger days, with adultery of the heart. Do we need to be more disciplined in this area?

At one time the Hebrews had adopted a mature attitude to their material goods. Their property and money had been plundered, but they had taken it calmly (10:34). How sad that they now needed to learn all over again how to be content with what they had. Christians ought to stand out against materialism. Jesus said that questions about what we should eat or wear are the sort of things that obsess the pagans (Matthew 6:25-34). In any case, verse 5 teaches that believers can be content because they are in the better situation. They have one who will never leave them, they have Jesus. When a child of God develops an unhealthy liking for things this is a sure sign that he has been seduced by the idea that money in the bank is a greater asset than the favour of God. Think it through: to parody verse 6, the materialist is really saying, 'Money is my helper, I will not fear what man can do to me.'

These verses echo the exhortation in 10:32: recall the *former days*. Twentieth century Christians take note. What a travesty it is if our former Christian life shames us.

Persevering in the way that we think (7-17)

As they cast their minds back to the early days of their service for Christ, the author encourages the Hebrew Christians to think about their first teachers in the things of God (7). Both their lives and their teaching are an encouragement to go on. Perhaps we too in our moments of trial would profit from looking back to the pastor or youth leader who helped bring us to faith. What would they think of us now? This is the background to the lovely statement in verse 8. Millions of believers have drawn solid comfort here. The author has a particular reason for saying it at this point. When we slide back, one of the worst problems is fear. It is corrosive. Suppose we did get back to a life of obedience; could we keep it up? Perhaps we have changed for the worst, and circumstances have altered too. In spite of all that, the Jesus who helped us in our yesterday, and who inspired the leaders we admired in days gone by, is still the same today. Who can tell what tomorrow will bring, but one thing is certain: Jesus will be no different.

Verse 9 reminds us that there is no place for novelty in the realm of Christian truth. The fad for something new takes many forms, but the author had an example in mind. In the first century, some thought that food could affect one's spiritual well being. Some people believed that eating Passover Lamb would benefit their souls as well as their bodies, whereas eating ordinary lamb would only nourish their bodies. In the same way, some people nowadays think that sacramental bread and

water can do something for the soul. This explains the statement in verse 10. The word *altar* is pictorial language. It tells us
that we depend on a sacrifice much greater than the ritual slaughter of bulls and goats. If we eat the meat of such animals it will
only affect the body but if we feed on Christ, this will bring
grace to the heart. Where do we stand on this? Do we depend
on some external ritual, or do we place our trust in what Jesus
did in giving his life for his people? This is where faith begins,
and if it is to grow it must stay rooted in the same soil. We will
never get beyond the need for simple trust.

Verses 11-13 take this further. In Old Testament days some
sacrifices were never eaten. This was the case with the sin-
offering. The carcass of the beast had to be burned outside the
camp. It was believed that the area where this took place was
defiled. In consequence, when Jesus died, he did so not in the
hallowed precincts of the temple, but outside the city on ground
polluted by its association with the ritual burning of carcasses
tainted by sin. The whole idea was offensive to pious Jews.
Nevertheless, the Cross of Jesus is where the Christian must
take his stand. This was the sticking point for many of the first
readers of this letter. Their Jewish contacts were disgusted by
Calvary. How could anyone follow a teacher who was clearly
under the curse of God? Real Christianity is always painful.
Take your stand alongside Jesus, and you will have to steel
yourself against the scorn and derision of a world that hates
him. Do you intend to follow Jesus? Do you mean to go with
him? Brace yourself. There is a reproach to be born.

Follow the picture through. Go to Calvary, and you turn
your back on the city. In spirit you say goodbye to all that it
stood for. Jerusalem was the centre of a religion whose day
had passed. It was not a *continuing city* (14), it had no future.
Something better was beckoning, a glorious existence in the
presence of God himself. No doubt it was hard for a person of
Jewish ancestry to leave Jerusalem and all its associations

behind him. In the same way, there are multitudes of believers who long for the old life, like the Israelites in Sinai longing for the leeks and garlic they left behind in Egypt. How unutterably sad. There is no comparison. Before you is Christ and all that he offers, behind you is a doomed and fading world. It is worth pressing on because of all that lies ahead. The believer has the advantage – he does not need blood sacrifices now. The perfect sacrifice of Christ has removed all that. The only sacrifices that are appropriate stem from a grateful heart: a mouth full of praise and a life full of good works and fellowship.

The New Testament never envisages private Christianity. If we are to go on, we cannot do so outside the local church. That is why the author counselled the Hebrews to place themselves under the discipline of godly elders (17). He had a horror of the kind of believer who is a law unto himself, the kind that are accountable to no one. There is no doubt that authority is a problem in church life, often because it is non-existent, occasionally because it is heavy-handed. Nevertheless, the disciple has a responsibility of his own. He is to submit. He must allow himself to be led, and taught, and cared for. In effect, the author tells us that we must not forget that those men who lead, teach and care for the churches face an awesome responsibility. The task is arduous. They *watch* over souls without regard to themselves. The picture is one of tireless care. They must do so knowing that God will demand an account one day. No wonder James warns us that those who aspire to be the teachers of God's people must be prepared for a *stricter judgement* than other Christians will receive (see James 3:1). The way that Christian people respond to those whom God has placed in authority over them cannot help but have an effect on these men. Some Christians are a grief to those who pastor them. Others are like the Philippians whom Paul said were his *joy and crown* (Philippians 4:1).

30
CLOSING WORDS

Please read Hebrews 13:18-25

A request for prayer (18-19)

We have now reached the closing stages of this epistle. The final verses of this letter are dominated by a prayer that the author offers for his readers. He begins however, by asking them to pray for him. First of all, this prayer tells us something about the first readers of this epistle. The very fact that the author wanted his friends to pray for him is a mighty encouragement. This is not the request of a man who thought that there was no hope for his readers. If he had been privately convinced that his readers had actually fallen away from the faith that they had once professed, he would not have requested their prayers. The prayers of apostates have no value. Such people do not get a hearing at *the throne of grace* (4:16). The first people to read those words, *pray for us*, must have been greatly relieved. By now there could be little doubt that the author was deeply troubled by the way that those Hebrew Christians had slipped back. If they took his warnings to heart there was ground to make up. Nevertheless, this artless request for prayer made it abundantly clear that he had not written them off completely. For all his undoubted concern, he still saw them as true believers and believed that their prayers could be used by God to bring blessing in his own situation.

Secondly, this prayer tells us something about the author himself. He refers in verse 18 to having *a good conscience* and a desire to live *honourably*. All that he had said so far in his epistle had been written out of honourable motives. Even though he had felt it necessary to give his friends some stern warnings, he had no need to reproach himself. At the same time, he clearly felt that he needed God's help. Again, this will have encouraged his readers. It is often tempting to suppose that Christian leaders are such elevated beings that they need no help from lesser mortals. How heartening then, to discover that the author did not put himself on a pedestal but saw himself as a Christian man on the same footing as other Christian men. He, like them, was weak and vulnerable and would need help from the Almighty. He would be greatly encouraged if his friends could seek that help from God just as they would be encouraged to know that he valued their prayers. And if the author of one of the books of the Bible needed his brothers and sisters to stand by him in prayer, how much more do ordinary Christian workers and indeed ordinary believers need prayer too. The prayer closes with a more specific request. He was clearly writing to people whom he knew personally and was longing to be re-united with them. He was confident that his prayers would help to bring this about.

A prayer for the Hebrews (20-21)

What follows is the author's own prayer for his readers. These words apply to those of us who read the epistle today as much as they did to those who read them in the first century. The prayer is really the conclusion to the whole epistle. The few verses that follow are really little more than a postscript. The prayer itself can be divided into three sections.

1. The God to whom we pray (20)

The first section concerns God himself (20). Who is this great being that we address in prayer? He is described first of all as *the God of peace*. This phrase is explained by the other phrases that follow later in verse 20, which refer to the Lord Jesus Christ and all that he achieved for his people through his death and resurrection. It is altogether remarkable that any human being could ever refer to a great and holy God as *the God of peace* because a state of war has existed between mankind and its maker for almost the whole of human history. By nature, our basic mindset is one of *enmity against God* (Romans 8:7). The message of the gospel however is that God is willing to be reconciled to his rebellious human creatures. This is only possible because Jesus shed his blood on behalf of sinners and was raised from the dead by his Father. For this reason, the Christian need no longer recoil from a God of wrath and offended majesty but may come into his presence with delighted astonishment, confident of his welcome. Sadly, this is not true of everybody. Some people, perhaps even some readers of this book, have yet to make their peace with God and are still *alienated and enemies* in their minds by *wicked works* (Colossians 1:21). This is nothing short of tragic when we reflect on the great pains that God has taken to be reconciled to sinners through the death of his Son.

Next we are told that God *brought up our Lord Jesus from the dead* (20). There could have been no resurrection however, if Jesus had not first submitted to death. The fact of Christ's death is also assumed in the phrase, *through the blood of the everlasting covenant* (20). We have here a forceful reminder that God is only to be at peace with men and women because Jesus, the great High Priest of his people also became the sacrificial victim who paid the price of their sins.

He was wounded for our transgressions, He was bruised for our iniquities; The chastisement for our peace was upon Him, And by His stripes we are healed. All we like sheep have gone astray; We have turned, every one, to his own way; And the LORD has laid on Him the iniquity of us all. (Isaiah 53:5-6)

The good shepherd gave his life for the sheep. The central great fact at the heart of the Christian gospel is that Jesus Christ, God's Son, was crucified for sinners. The Hebrew believers who were the very first people to have read these words will not have missed the author's reason for reminding them of the great event that lies at the heart of the gospel. Nor should we. All that Jesus did and suffered at Calvary demands a response.

> Were the whole realm of nature mine,
> That were an offering far too small;
> Love so amazing, so divine,
> Demands my soul, my life, my all.

> (Isaac Watts, 1674-1748)

Having died as the substitute for his people, Jesus rose from the dead. It is a curious fact that this is the only reference to the resurrection of Jesus in the whole epistle. The Bible sometimes speaks of Jesus' resurrection as though it were something that he accomplished by his own power. *Jesus .... said to them, 'Destroy this temple, and in three days I will raise it up.' .... He was speaking of the temple of His body.* (John 2:19, 21) Here, by contrast, we are told that God raised him up. The resurrection of the Son of God was an extraordinary act of divine power, a miracle like no other. At this stage however, the author is not so much concerned to emphasise the resurrection as a display of colossal might but rather as an act of justice. Jesus was raised from the dead *through the blood of the everlasting covenant.* It is called the *everlasting covenant* to distinguish it from other covenants, made with the people of Israel, which were purely temporary, especially the one made at Sinai (described as the *first covenant* in 8:7). It refers to the covenant made in eternity between God the Father and God the Son, that the Son would act as mediator between a holy God and a sinful people. That covenant was ultimately ratified in blood at Calvary. Though he was not the covenant breaker, out of love for his people, Jesus took the curse of the covenant upon himself. By his death, the honour of God was satisfied, his justice was vindicated, sin was punished and a penalty was paid in full. It was therefore a moral necessity that Jesus should be raised from the dead. Death had no claim on him. The Lord Christ was raised from death not merely because God is stronger than sin and the grave but also because it was fitting and right that one who had fulfilled his commission as the mediator of his people and *became obedient to the point of death* (Philippians 2:8) should be exalted to the highest place.

In view of all that he achieved in his death and resurrection, it is not surprising that the author refers to Lord Jesus as *that great shepherd of the sheep* (20). In the Old Testament, God is described as the *shepherd of Israel*, leading his people like a flock (Psalm 80:1). First and foremost however, there is an echo here of Jesus description of himself as the *good shepherd* (John 10:7-30). When Jesus described himself in that way (John 10:11, 14) he meant to emphasise the word 'good'. It translates a Greek word, which means excellent or beautiful. Jesus said, in effect, 'I am the shepherd, the good one' as though to draw a contrast between himself and every other shepherd. Not only is he the leader, the guide and the protector of his flock, as all shepherds are called to be, but he is also a shepherd of unique quality. Unlike any other shepherd, he gave his life for the sheep. There is a tender bond between a shepherd and his sheep. Already in this epistle the author has used a number of terms to illustrate this. Who are the sheep of Christ's flock? They are those who *will inherit salvation* (1:14), the *many sons* whom the *captain of their salvation* will bring *to glory* (2:10), the *holy brethren* of Messiah and *partakers of the heavenly calling* (3:1), the *heirs of promise* (6:17) and those who will receive *a kingdom which cannot be shaken* (12:28). It is no small matter to be one of the sheep of Christ's flock. There is no higher privilege, no greater blessing. The author was originally prompted to write this letter because he feared that the Hebrew Christians were in danger of falling away from the faith they had once professed. In verse 20 he reminded his friends just how much they had. The God of Israel was at peace with them. The Christ they had come to embrace had died in their place to ratify a covenant that would never be revoked and had been raised to glory. They had Christ for their shepherd, a shepherd like no other. They themselves had become his beloved sheep. What an incentive to persevere! And we too should resist the pressure to turn back to the old life. With such a God, such a saviour and such a glorious salvation, there could be no greater folly.

2. A prayer for wavering Christians (21)

The author prayed that the wonderful God he had described so movingly in verse 20 would make his friends *complete*. We meet the same word in Ephesians 4:13, where we read that the risen Christ *gave some to be apostles, some prophets, some evangelists, and some pastors and teachers, for the **equipping** of the saints for the work of ministry ...* (Ephesians 4:11-12). In effect, he prayed that God would supply them with those qualities that they lacked in order to make them fit for his service. It was a prayer for greater maturity, for a more robust Christian testimony. Believers who had showed a worrying tendency to instability needed to make progress. They needed to develop a well-rounded Christian character with no glaring weaknesses. That is why the author is so comprehensive in his prayer. He wanted God to make his friends *complete in every good work.* They were not merely to do the will of God in a partial and limited way, but to bring the whole of their lives into conformity with it. They needed God's help to bring every faculty of mind and body and every area of life to the point where all of it was *well pleasing in his sight.* This is an ambitious prayer, but those first century believers needed no less and neither do we. It is a daunting task to bring *every thought into captivity to the obedience of Christ* (2 Corinthians 10:5) and to please God in all that we do in all the varied situations that we meet. Modern Christians would do well to pray for one another in the same way that the author prayed for his friends.

3. The ultimate goal of all our prayers (21)

The author's prayer concludes with an ascription of praise to the Lord Jesus Christ. First of all, prayer is offered *through* him. If it were not for Jesus, prayer would be impossible. If Jesus, as the *great shepherd of the sheep* had not shed his blood on behalf of his people, if God had not raised him from the dead, a state of enmity would still exist between God and man. There would be no true Christians. The entire human race would be estranged from God and no communication from man to God would be possible. It is only because of Jesus that prayer can ever take place. There is also a sense in which prayer is for Jesus Christ. The great object of prayer is the glory of Christ. The author of this epistle wanted God to lead his friends on to greater maturity so that Christ might be glorified by it. If those first century believers were to fall away, it would reflect badly on the reputation of our Saviour. His power to save to the utmost would be called into question. It was therefore extremely important that God should intervene in their lives and enable them to make up the ground they had lost and advance to greater levels of Christian discipleship. The glory of his Son was at stake. This same perspective would do a great deal to revolutionise the prayer lives of modern Christians and the effectiveness of our Church prayer meetings. We need to repent of the self-centredness of much of our praying and focus instead on crying to God to magnify the name of his Son. The Lord Christ is supremely worthy of it!

The author's postscript (22-25)

The epistle closes with a brief postscript from the author. He begins with a tender appeal to the Hebrew believers, addressing them as *brethren* (22). The fact that he was their brother gave him certain rights, including the right to deal with them in a way that was frank and bold. He had written out of concern for them and been faithful in expressing his concerns. Neverthe-less, his concern had been prompted by love and he expressed the hope that they would *bear with the word of exhortation*, in other words, that they would take it kindly and receive his words in the spirit in which he had written them.

It is clear from verse 23 that Timothy, who had been groomed as a Christian leader by the apostle Paul, was known both to the author and his readers. We know nothing of the circum-stances that led to his release from imprisonment, but the author had no doubt that this good news would encourage Christians everywhere, including those who received this letter.

Verse 24 gives a closing greeting, first to the elders of the church (*those who rule over you*) and to the believers in general (*all the saints*). The phrase *those from* Italy is not at all clear in the original, which reads something like 'those who are from or of Italy'. We cannot therefore be sure whether it refers to people living in Italy or people of Italian extraction. It is probably best to read it as 'greetings from our Italian friends.' With this in mind, there is no hard evidence in this verse to suggest that the epistle was written in Italy.

The closing benediction in verse 25 is very short, *Grace be with you all, Amen.* The first readers of this epistle would understand that these few words actually contain a great deal of truth. The author longed that his friends might know the grace of God, his free, unmerited favour, his kindness to the undeserving. This is mediated only through the Christ who features so prominently in this letter and who tasted death for his people (2:9). It originates at the throne of grace (4:16) where help is available to all the people of God in their hour of need. It is this grace which establishes the hearts of believers (13:9) and keeps all the people of God through every trial until at last we see what we have long hoped for, the city that God has prepared for his own (11:16). If we have nothing more than the grace of God, we will need nothing more.

APPENDIX

A word about books

This book has an essentially modest purpose. I hope and pray that anyone who reads it will understand the epistle to the Hebrews more fully than he did at the outset. I wanted to convey something of the urgency of the epistle's message, that Christianity is a serious business, that in Christ we have a great saviour and that those who follow Jesus must *run with endurance the race that is set before us* (12:1). Even so, in writing this volume I did not set out to right an exhaustive commentary. For those who would like to take a deeper dip into the riches of this small part of the word of God I would recommend the following books.

First of all, Geoffrey B. Wilson has written a number of books on the New Testament epistles. He has called them 'Digests of Reformed Comment'. Each one takes the reader through the epistle in question, looking at each verse in turn. Instead of commenting on the verses himself, Mr Wilson has gathered a selection of quotations from the works of great Bible scholars. Although these books are small, and therefore attractively priced, they are crammed with good things. Serious Bible students ought to consider acquiring not only the volume on Hebrews, but also the entire set. It would be money well spent. These books are produced by the Banner of Truth Trust. Inter Varsity Press have published a number of helpful titles, one is in 'Bible Speaks Today' series and was written by Raymond Brown. It is subtitled *Christ above all.* Another, in their series of Tyndale Commentaries, is by Donald Guthrie. IVP also publish a volume on Hebrews by Ray C. Stedman in their New Testament Commentary series,. An excellent, not to say outstanding 'heavyweight' commentary is the one written by Philip Edgecumbe Hughes and published by Eerdmans. I found this work to be extremely helpful both in the preparation of sermons and in the writing of this book. Two classic commentaries from an earlier age are also worthy of note. The first is by Dr John Brown, a Scots minister active in the nineteenth century. His work is painstaking and thorough and at the same time, devotional and warm-hearted. It is published by the Banner of Truth Trust in their Geneva series of Commentaries. The second of the two is both larger and more demanding. The Banner of Truth Trust also publishes in seven volumes the commentary by Dr John Owen, the seventeenth English Puritan. John Owen was a giant in an age of giants. This magisterial work would certainly repay careful study, but would also call for a large outlay both in time and money.

While it is not a commentary and doesn't set out to be one, *God's Hall of Fame* by Peter Lewis is a stimulating and heartwarming survey of the portrait gallery of the heroes of faith in Hebrews 11. It is published by Christian Focus Publications. Faith, we are told, is *the substance of things hoped for* (11:1). In Hebrews, faith is often held up as the ability to place our trust not so much in what God has done for us in Christ but in what he will do for us in the future. One book that will certainly help to strengthen the believer's confidence as he looks ahead into the unknown is *Future Grace* John Piper, published in the USA by Multnomah Books and in the UK by IVP.

NO TURNING BACK

At various points in this book I have observed that certain features of modern Christianity have helped to replicate the situation that troubled the author of the epistle. In part this is because a form of evangelism became prevalent in the nineteenth and twentieth centuries that encouraged people to decide for Christ in a way that sometimes stopped short of true conversion. One small book that will help to introduce this subject is *Today's Gospel: Authentic or Synthetic?* by Walter J. Chantry, published by the Banner of Truth. Another helpful book that explores this issue is *The Gospel According to Jesus* by John F. MacArthur Jr, published by Zondervan. The subtitle explains the message of the book, *What does Jesus mean when he says follow me?* I would also strongly recommend *Revival and Revivalism: The Making and Marring of American Evangelicalism 1750-1859* by Iain H. Murray, which is published by the Banner of Truth Trust. This is a book that helps to explain how modern Evangelicalism has drifted from its biblical moorings.

How sure the scriptures are!
God's vital, urgent word,
as true as steel, and far
more sharp than any sword:
so deep and fine,
at his control
they pierce where soul
and spirit join.

They test each human thought,
refining like a fire;
they measure what we ought
to do and to desire:
for God knows all –
exposed it lies
before his eyes
to whom we call.

Let those who hear his voice
confronting them today
reject the tempting choice
of doubting or delay:
for God speaks still – his word is clear,
so let us hear
and do his will!

Author: Christopher Idle (1938-)
Copyright: Christopher Idle / Jubilate Hymns

SOME OF THE TITLES PUBLISHED BY GRACE PUBLICATIONS TRUST

Nick Needham

2000 Years of Christ's Power – part one – The Age of the Church Fathers

2000 Years of Christ's Power – part two – The Middle Ages

'fascinating to read and hard to leave down – warmly commended' – (Frederick S. Leahy, Banner of Truth magazine).

Clifford Pond

Autumn Gold

'This is a book which every person over sixty should read' – (James Kerr, Covenanter Witness).

Frank Allred

How Can I Be Sure?

'A valuable addition to any home or church library' – (Peace and Truth)

The Eclipse of the Gospel – an assessment of the gospel in today's church

'essential reading for every man that enters the pulpit' – (Our Inheritance).

Fix Your Eyes on Jesus (a forthcoming title from GPT).

Other books by Phil Arthur

Patience of Hope – a Welwyn Commentary on 1&2 Thessalonians – published by Evangelical Press